A Drawing a Day

Unlock your inner artist

Tamara Michael

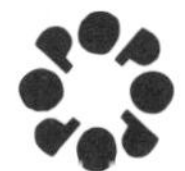

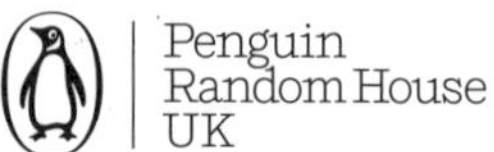

Pop Press

UK | USA | Canada | Ireland | Australia
India | New Zealand | South Africa

Pop Press is part of the Penguin Random House group of companies whose addresses can be found at
global.penguinrandomhouse.com

Penguin Random House UK
One Embassy Gardens, 8 Viaduct Gardens, London SW11 7BW

penguin.co.uk
global.penguinrandomhouse.com

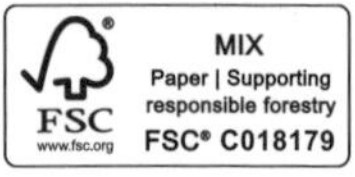

Penguin
Random House
UK

First published by Pop Press in 2025

1 2 3 4 5 6 7 8 9 10

Text and Illustrations © Tamara Michael

Cover illustrations by Tamara Michael
Cover design by Loulou Clark © Ebury Publishing
Internal design by Adam Laszczuk © Penguin Random House Australia Pty Ltd
Typeset in 12/17pt Bustani by Post Pre-press Group, Australia

Printed and bound in Malaysia by Times Offset SDN BHD.

The authorised representative in the EEA is Penguin Random House Ireland, Morrison Chambers, 32 Nassau Street, Dublin D02 YH68.

A CIP catalogue record for this book is available from the British Library

ISBN 9781529955316

Contents

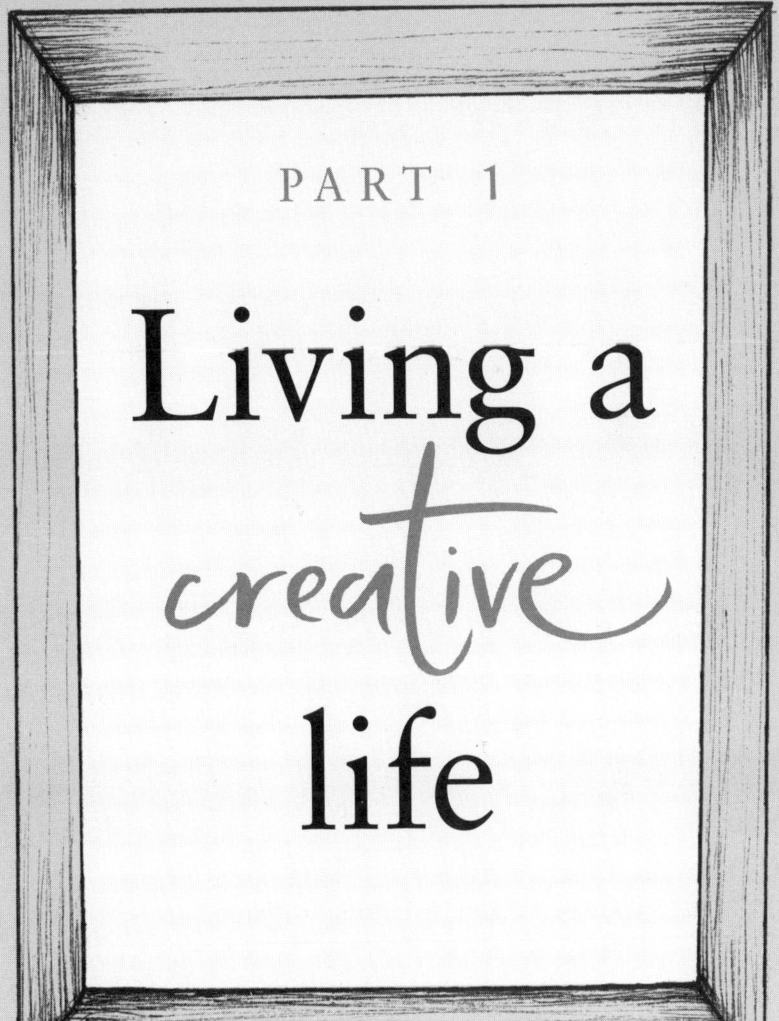

PART 1
Living a
creative
life

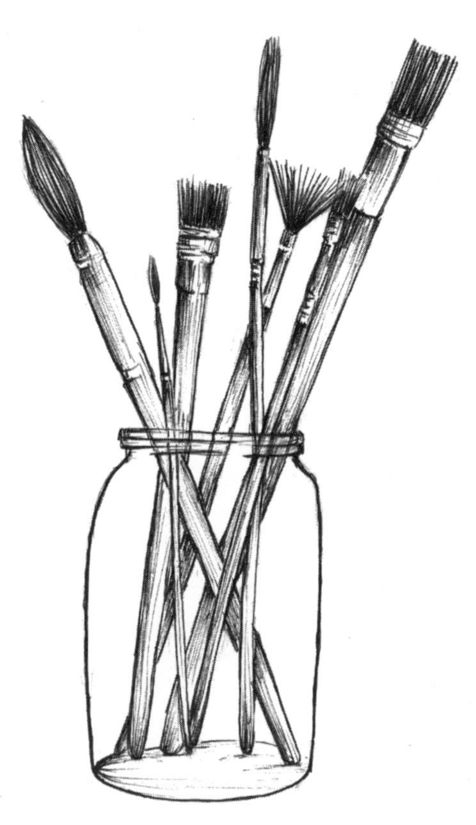

It's a common belief that only some people are born with the gift of creativity; that you're either blessed with the ability to draw or you are not. This couldn't be further from the truth.

Creativity is a skill that can be learnt, just like any other. Living a creative life means embracing the idea that everyone has the potential to be imaginative and inventive – yes, even you! It involves nurturing your curiosity, exploring what creativity means to you and allowing yourself the freedom to experiment without the fear of failure. It's about finding inspiration in everyday moments and expressing your unique perspective through various mediums and art forms. A creative life is a journey of continuous learning and self-expression that deepens your connection with the world and yourself.

There's no right or wrong way to draw. Yes, there are rules and conventions that make drawing easier but they are simply guidelines. True creativity is never limited by the rules and procedures – it exists beyond their confines. It just is.

If you have ever observed a child drawing, you know exactly what I mean. A child doesn't pick up a pencil and ask, 'What is the best composition for this drawing?' They just begin. They let creativity flow through them and simply draw what they see or imagine, in whatever form it takes. That is the essence of living a creative life – tapping into that childlike wonder of drawing, of creating for the sake of it, and reaping the benefits that come from it.

The purpose of this book is not to teach you how to draw like me but to play with the exercises to develop your own drawing style. I want you to use this book as a tool to uncover the creative powers that already exist within you. Explore the techniques and activities in these pages and let them inspire you to create in your own way.

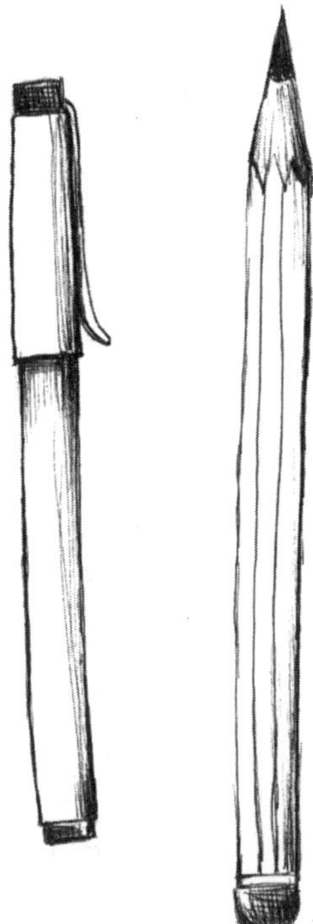

The *benefits* of art on mental health

Engaging in art can offer profound benefits for mental health. Art provides a sanctuary in today's fast-paced world. When you immerse yourself in creating, you enter a state of flow. This state, where you are fully absorbed in what you're doing, can help quiet the mind and reduce anxiety.

Research in neuroscience has increasingly highlighted the significant benefits of engaging in creative arts for brain health and function. Creative activities have been found to enhance various aspects of cognitive and emotional wellbeing. Here are some key findings from recent studies.

Cognitive benefits

Enhanced neural connectivity

Engaging in creative arts can enhance connectivity between different areas in the brain that are involved in internal thought processes such as daydreaming, memory retrieval and envisioning the future.

Improved executive function

Creative activities can improve higher order thinking skills including problem solving, planning and multi-tasking. This is due to the requirement for sustained attention, memory and coordination during these activities.

Neuroplasticity

The brain is an amazing organ! It has the ability to reorganise itself by forming new neural connections. This is known as neuroplasticity. Engaging in creative activities promotes neuro-plasticity, which can help in brain recovery from conditions like stroke and in slowing cognitive decline in ageing.

Emotional benefits

Stress reduction

Participating in the creative arts has been shown to reduce levels of cortisol, the hormone related to stress. Activities like painting, drawing and music can serve as effective outlets for expressing emotions and reducing stress and anxiety.

Enhanced mood and wellbeing

Engaging in art practices helps modulate emotions, which positively influences mood and promotes self-compassion. Creative activities can help individuals access and process emotions like fear and joy, to release pent-up emotion. They also activate the systems responsible for positive mood states and motivation.

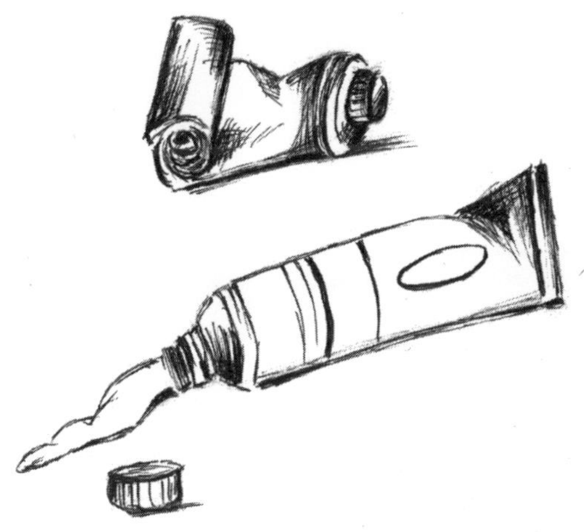

The *myth* of perfection

Perfectionism has been my biggest enemy in my art journey and is something many artists struggle with. This idea that every line must be flawless and each piece be a masterpiece is not only unrealistic but it also stifles creativity. Art is fundamentally about self-expression and exploration. When you fixate on perfection, you miss out on the joy of discovery and the learning that comes from making mistakes.

The truth is, in art-making these 'mistakes' are essential – they often lead to unexpected and unique results that can enhance your work in ways you never imagined. Embracing imperfection allows you to experiment freely, develop your own style and grow as an artist.

Instead of striving for perfection in your drawings, focus on the process and the emotions you want to convey. Every piece you create, no matter how imperfect, is a step forward in your artistic journey.

THIS IS A DRAWING OF AN APPLE.

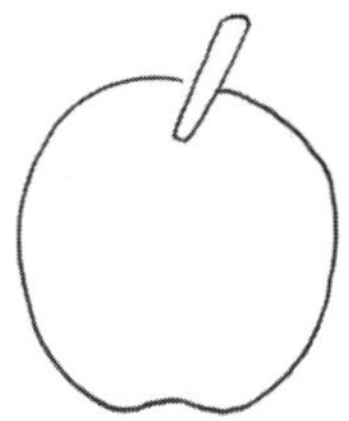

THIS IS A DRAWING OF AN APPLE.

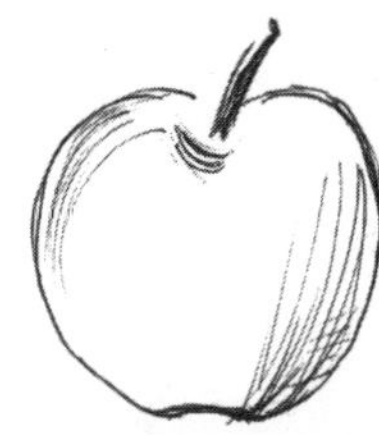

THIS IS ALSO A DRAWING OF AN APPLE.

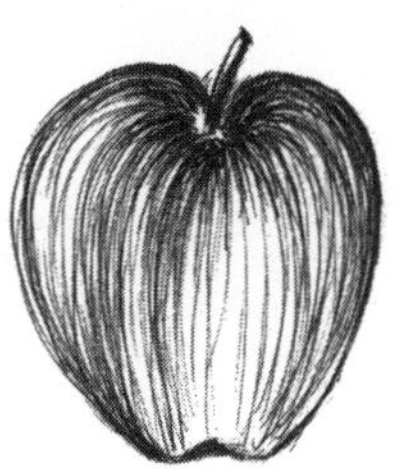

They are each perfect in their own way. Your unique style and the flair you add to each drawing you create are what makes your artwork yours!

Let's draw!

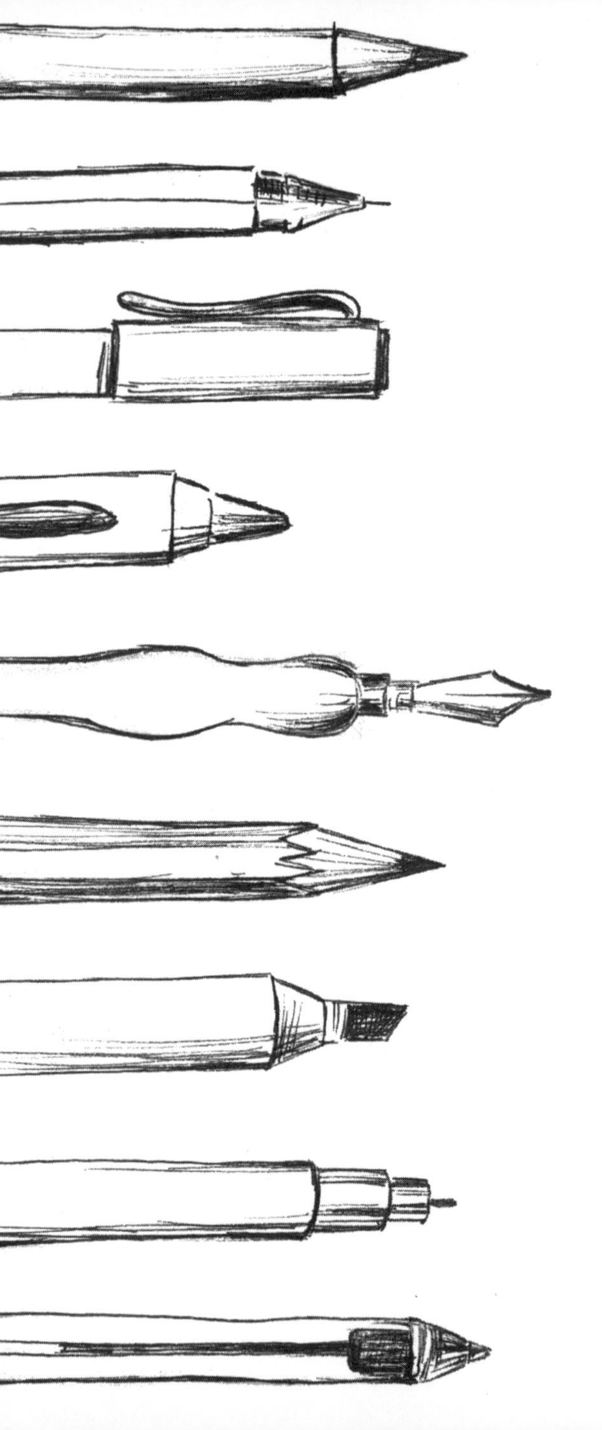

The *difference* between doodling and drawing

Incorporating art into your routine doesn't have to be complicated. Start with something simple: a doodle in the margin of your notebook, a quick sketch of a flower or even colouring in an existing pattern. The key is to start. Don't worry about the end result or whether it's 'good' or 'bad'. The act of creating is what matters most.

My previous book, *A Doodle a Day*, provides a series of doodling prompts, whereas this book focuses on drawing. What's the difference? While they both involve putting pen to paper, they serve different purposes and bring unique joys.

Doodling is often seen as the art of the subconscious. It describes the act of generating spontaneous scribbles and shapes that appear in the margins of your notebook during a meeting or a phone call. Doodling doesn't usually follow a rigid plan or strive for perfection. It's carefree, unstructured and often done without much thought. It's about letting your mind wander and your hand move spontaneously, allowing free expression of whatever comes out in the moment.

Drawing, on the other hand, is a bit more intentional. It involves planning and a certain level of focus. When you draw, you might have a specific subject in mind and the intention to capture this on the page involves taking a more structured approach. Drawing can be detailed and precise or loose and expressive, but it generally follows some kind of plan or vision. Nevertheless, although drawing might involve more direction and structure, remember that rules are made to be broken. Don't let your drawing practice be hindered or limited by the 'rules' you've learnt along the way; they are simply there to guide you.

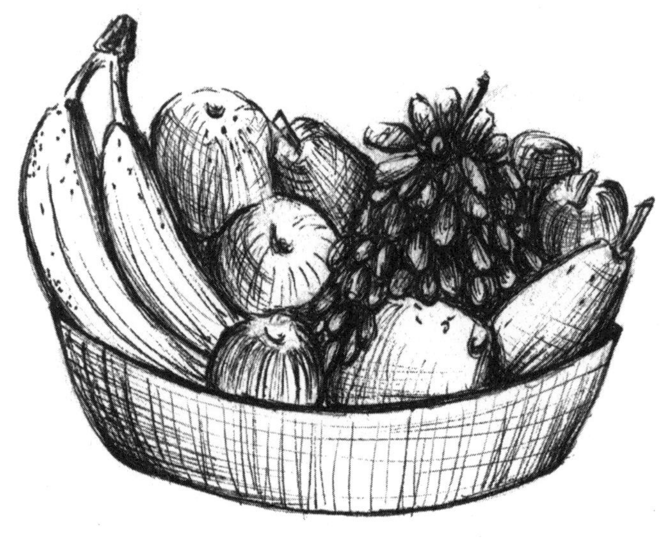

Drawing tools

When it comes to drawing, there's no need to stick to just using a pencil. The beauty of art lies in the freedom to experiment and play with whatever tools you have at hand. I usually begin with a pencil sketch – it feels like a safe starting point – but from there, anything goes. I love the bold, dynamic look of fineliners and markers; they make lines pop in ways that pencil just can't. Others might prefer the smudgy softness of charcoal or the subtle gradients of graphite.

There's no wrong choice here. Try everything. Pick up a pen, a marker, or even a piece of chalk if that's what's nearby. Every tool has its own quirks, its own way of helping you see and express the world. Maybe you'll fall in love with the effortless glide of a gel pen. Who knows? The important thing is to let your curiosity guide you. Let's explore a few tools.

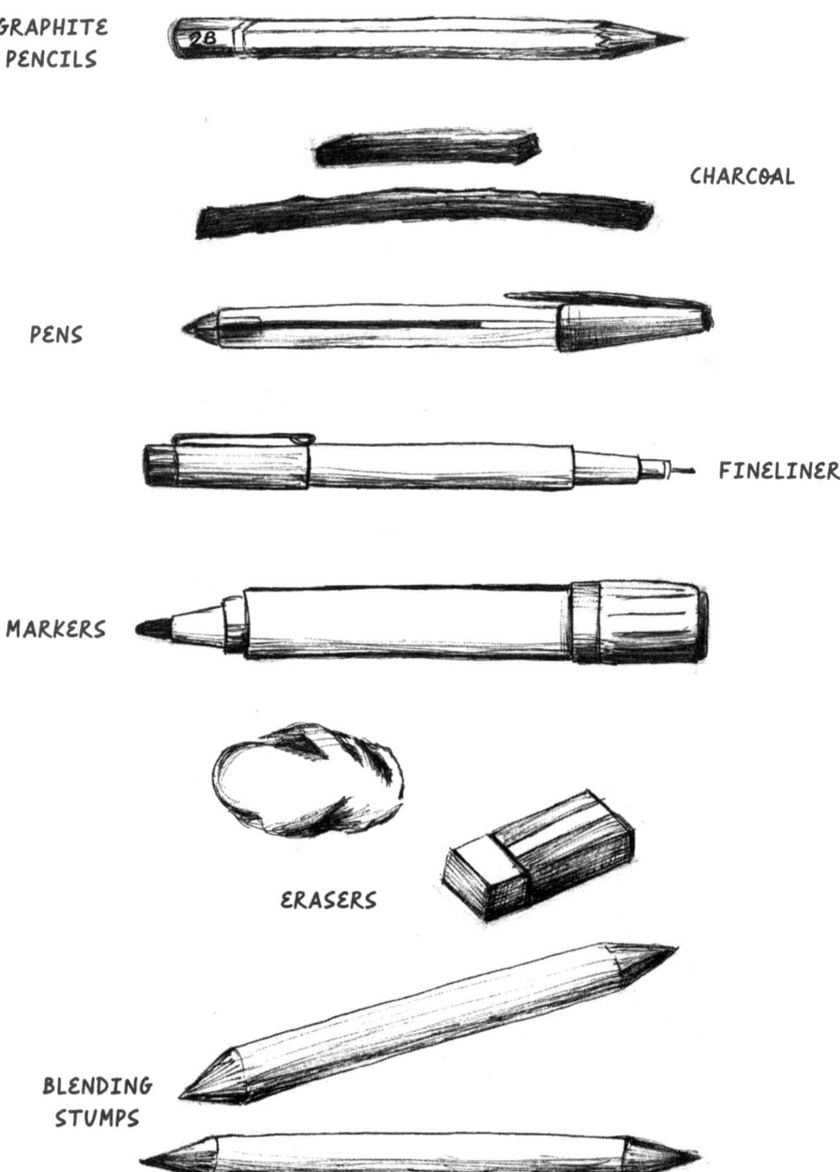

GRAPHITE PENCILS
2B
CHARCOAL
PENS
FINELINERS
MARKERS
ERASERS
BLENDING STUMPS

Graphite pencils

Graphite pencils are the most common drawing tool. They're perfect for when you're feeling detail oriented or want to ease into shading. Drawing pencils come in various grades, from 9H (hardest) to 9B (softest). Hard pencils (H grades) produce light, fine lines ideal for details, while soft pencils (B grades) create darker, broader strokes suitable for shading and bold lines.

Charcoal

Charcoal is a versatile drawing medium known for its rich, deep blacks and quick coverage. It's perfect for creating drama and movement in a drawing. Charcoal comes in three main types: vine/willow charcoal (soft, powdery and easily erasable), compressed charcoal (dense and intense) and charcoal pencils (convenient for detail work and available in tints). Charcoal is excellent for expressive, dramatic drawings due to its smudge capability and its ability to create bold contrasts.

Pens

Drawing pens, including ballpoint and gel pens, provide a consistent ink flow for smooth, precise lines. They are great for adding details and outlines and for offering a permanent mark that doesn't smudge easily.

Fineliners

These are specialised pens with a very fine, consistent tip, often used for detailed line work and technical drawing. They come in various tip sizes, allowing for a range of line widths. Fineliners are popular for their precision and their ability to create crisp, clean lines.

Markers

Markers come in a wide array of colours and tip sizes, from broad chisel tips to fine points. They are excellent for bold, vibrant drawings and are often used in graphic design and illustration.

Erasers

Erasers are essential for correcting mistakes and creating highlights in drawings. Kneaded erasers are pliable and can be shaped to lift graphite or charcoal cleanly. Vinyl or plastic erasers are firmer and more precise, ideal for detailed erasing.

Blending stumps

Blending stumps (sometimes called stubs) are tools used to blend and smudge graphite or charcoal to create smooth transitions and shading. They are typically made of compressed paper or soft leather rolled into a cylindrical shape. Blending stumps help create gradual gradients and soften harsh lines, enhancing the overall texture and depth of your drawing.

Drawing techniques

Drawing is all about layers – layers of shapes, layers of lines, layers of shading. Start with a light touch and let the shapes and shadows build slowly. Here are a few things to keep in mind as you practise.

Light

Light is crucial in drawing because it defines how objects appear. In drawing, we use shading to show the different light values. When thinking about light in drawing, consider the following:

Light source

Always decide where your light source is coming from; imagine where the sun or a light bulb might be in relation to the object you're drawing. This will help you determine where the highlights and shadows fall.

Highlights

These are the brightest spots on your drawing where the light hits directly. Keep these areas lighter.

Shadows

Opposite to highlights, shadows are the darkest areas where the light is blocked. Use shading techniques to create these areas.

Mid-tones

These are the in-between values that transition between light and dark. Use a lighter touch of your shading technique to show the transition between light and dark.

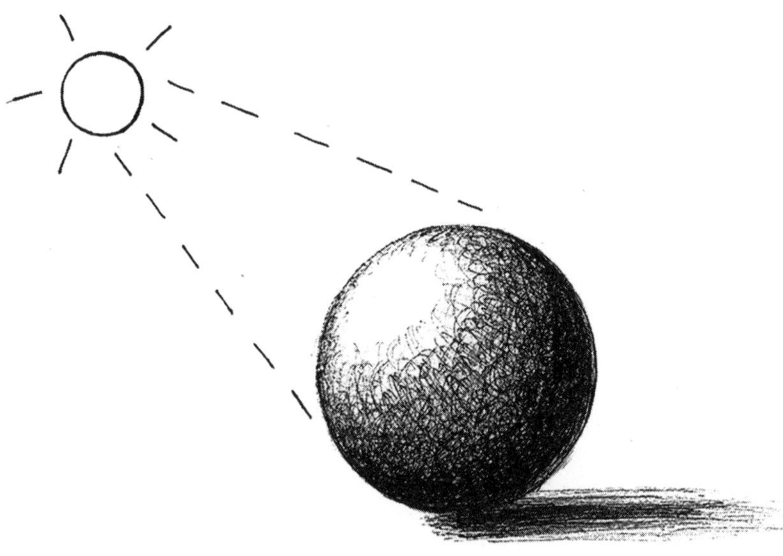

Shading

Shading is what gives your sketches depth and dimension and is how you show the light and shadow on an object. As you work through the drawing prompts in this book, experiment with using each shading style. Start by creating really dark and dense shading then go lighter and more spread out. Use whatever drawing tool you're comfortable with.

Here are some easy ways to generate shading:

Hatching

This involves drawing closely spaced parallel lines. The closer the lines, the darker the area will appear.

Cross-hatching

Similar to hatching, but you add another set of parallel lines that cross the first set. This technique is great for creating a richer, darker shadow.

Scumbling

Creates a textured effect by using small, circular or scribbled strokes, often to build up layers and add depth and richness to an area of a drawing.

Stippling

Involves using small dots. The idea is to control the spacing of the dots to create different levels of shading and texture. When the dots are placed close together, they create darker, more solid areas; when spaced further apart, they give the impression of lighter tones.

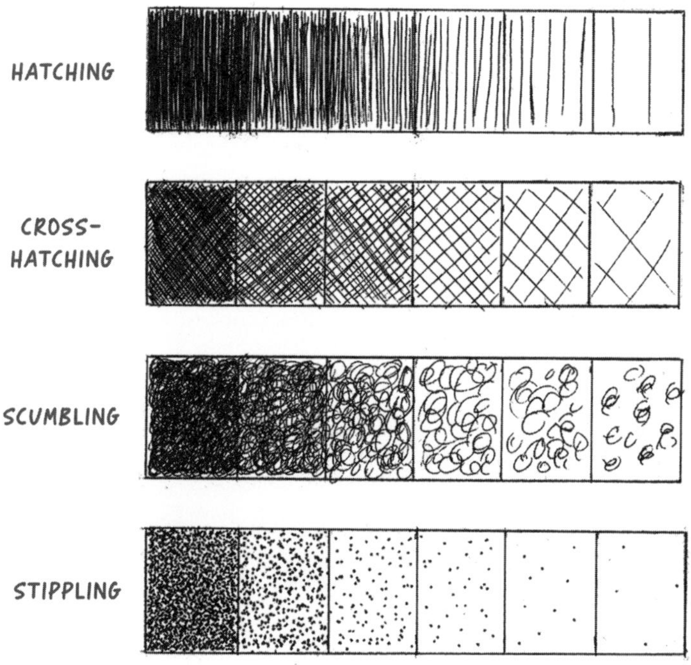

Try out each shading style in the boxes below.
Start with really dark and dense shading
then progress to light and spread out.
Use whatever drawing tool you're comfortable with.

HATCHING

CROSS-
HATCHING

SCUMBLING

STIPPLING

Add shading detail to this ball based on where the light is coming from. Remember: highlights are where the sun hits the ball and shadows are where the light is blocked. Use any of the shading techniques described in the previous pages. Hint: start light and build up slowly to the darkest layer.

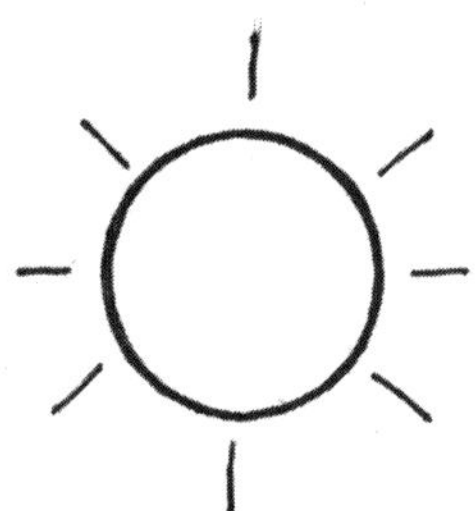

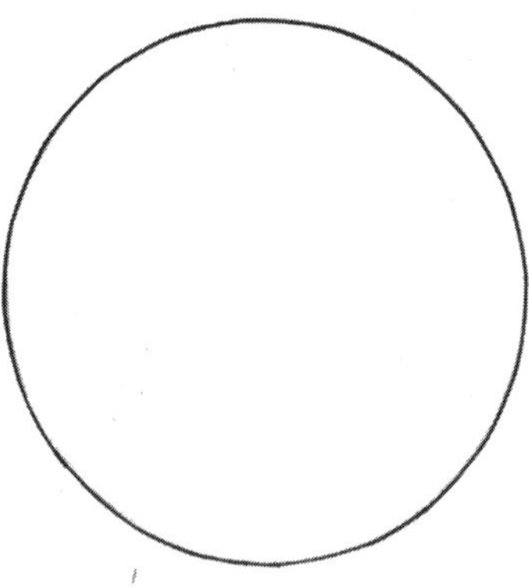

Finding the shapes

One of the fundamentals of drawing is finding the basic shapes that make up the subject you are trying to draw. This will help you strip back the details of what you are drawing and help you focus on shapes, shadows and contrasts.

Observe your subject

Before you put pencil to paper, take a moment to look closely at what you're drawing. Whether it's a person, an animal or an object, try to see it as a collection of basic shapes. This will help you break down the complexity into manageable parts.

Identify and draw the basic shapes

Most things you want to draw can be simplified into basic shapes like circles, ovals, rectangles, squares and triangles. Although it might be tempting to jump straight in, it is worth starting with these basic shapes as they will help you get the proportions and placement right. Use a light hand when you sketch these shapes so you can easily erase and adjust as needed.

For example, if I were to draw a mug I could simplify it into the basic shapes of a rectangle for the body, an oval for the mouth and a curved shape for the handle.

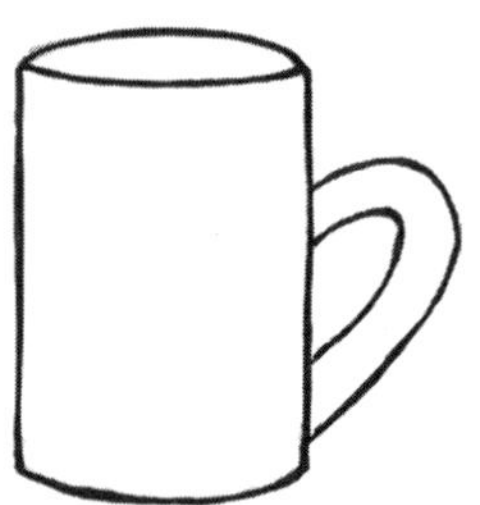

Refine the outline

Once you have your basic shapes, you can begin to refine your outline. Look at your subject again and adjust the shapes and lines to more closely match what you see. Start adding in smaller details as you go.

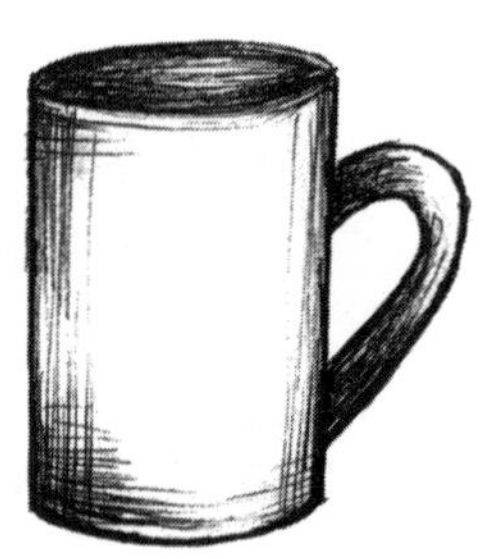

Add details

With your basic outline complete, you can start adding further details to create depth. This includes adding shadows, contrasts, textures and any other specific characteristics of your subject. Keep building up your drawing gradually, step by step.

Tips for *success!*

Observe and simplify

Break down complex objects into simple geometric shapes like circles, squares, rectangles and triangles. Look for the fundamental shapes that make up the overall structure of your subject.

Use light, loose lines

Start with light, loose lines to sketch the basic shapes and outlines. This allows you to easily adjust proportions and placements before committing to darker, more defined lines.

Build up gradually

Start with the largest and most prominent shapes first, then gradually add smaller shapes and details. This helps maintain the overall structure and balance of your sketch as you refine it.

Drawing styles

Loose drawing

Loose drawing is my favourite form of drawing. It breaks a lot of the rules I went through in the previous section and it allows for more free and relaxed artistic expression. It is an artistic technique that prioritises fluidity, spontaneity and expressiveness over precision and detail. It involves creating quick, free-form sketches that capture the essence, movement and energy of a subject rather than focusing on exact replication. This style of drawing encourages you to use swift, broad strokes, often resulting in dynamic and lively drawings.

Creating loose drawings involves drawing sweeping lines rather than focusing on tight movements, allowing your strokes to be more fluid and expressive. This style of drawing is a great way to convey mood and emotion rather than strict realism.

Loose drawing can incorporate a variety of lines, which help convey movement, texture and shape.

Line variation: Try different types of lines – straight, curved, zigzag and wavy. This helps loosen up your handand allows you to get comfortable with free-form shapes.

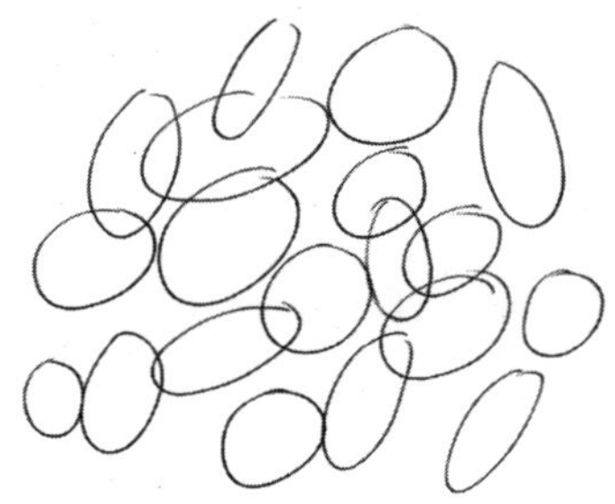

Circular motions: Draw quick, overlapping circles and ovals. Focus on speed and fluidity rather than precision.

Continuous line drawing

Continuous line drawing involves keeping your pen or pencil on the page and allowing your hand to continue to move freely across the page as you draw. This style helps create a dynamic artwork full of movement and flow.

Let's practise this technique:

1. Set a timer for 5–10 minutes. This will encourage you to work quickly and avoid getting bogged down in details.

2. Create a drawing of a flower without lifting your pen or pencil from the paper. This encourages a focus on the overall composition and flow of lines. You can work off real life examples or search for images online.

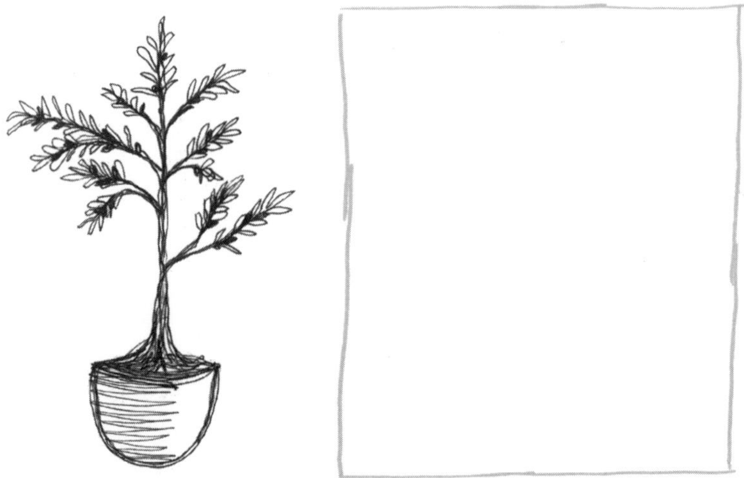

Blind contour drawing

Blind contour drawing is a fun and challenging exercise that involves drawing your subject without looking at the paper. This style of drawing embraces imperfection – it is not going to look pretty, as you can see from my drawings of a guitar and a vase with flowers. This exercise enhances your observation skills and helps you trust your hand–eye coordination.

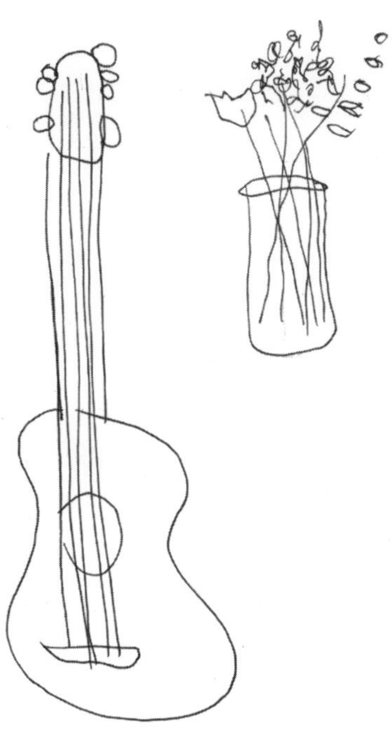

Challenge exercise!

Draw an object you have
in your bag or on your
deskwithout looking at
the paper, focusing only
on the contours and
shapes you see.

Tips for success!

Keep your hand moving

Avoid resting your hand on the paper for too long.
Keep it moving to maintain fluidity in your lines.

Embrace imperfections

Loose drawing is about capturing the essence, so don't
worry about mistakes. Imperfections can add character
and expressiveness.

Judgement-free drawing

Imagine yourself as a kid again, putting pen to paper with nothing to prove, just seeing where it takes you. Each line, each squiggle, is like a little echo of what you're feeling right now – good, bad, messy or calm. When you're drawing without judgement, you're not trying to make art that's impressive; you're just allowing yourself to create. Judgement-free drawing is about letting go of control and letting your hand move, with no expectations and no need to fix anything.

One way to get started is to set a timer and give yourself permission to draw without lifting your pen, even if it feels strange or silly. Breathe . . . and let yourself enjoy the unexpected. Let each line, curve or mistake be what it is – a small piece of how you see the world in this exact moment. When you draw like this, you let yourself be human: imperfect, open and free.

Five-minute drawing exercises

Now that you've explored some simple drawing techniques, let's put them into practice. I've included some simple prompt outlines to inspire you but I encourage you to experiment using a variety of drawing styles and techniques. You can draw from real-life references or from images you may find online. Remember, this book is only a guide. The power is in your hands to turn these drawings into whatever you want.

There is no expectation that you complete these drawings in five minutes; this is just a suggestion to get you started. Ultimately, the goal is to feel relaxed and stay in the moment as you draw. Setting a timer might help you let go of distractions and focus on the task or it might really stress you out! Do what feels right and enjoy the process of creating.

Textures

Wood grain

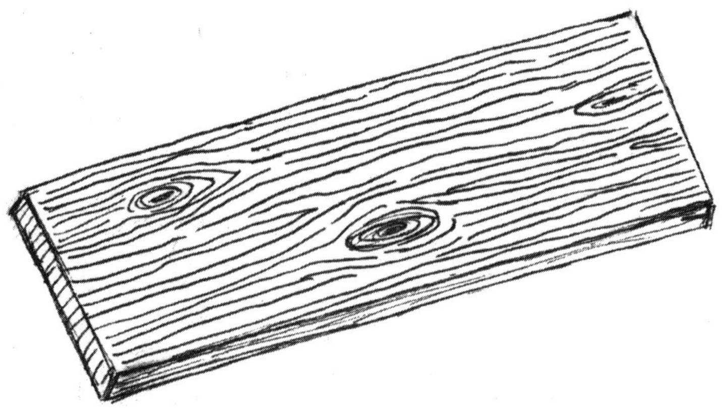

Bricks

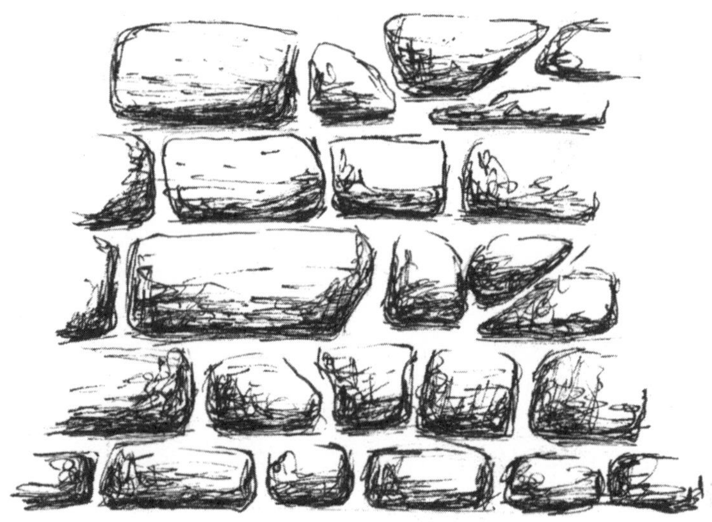

Water

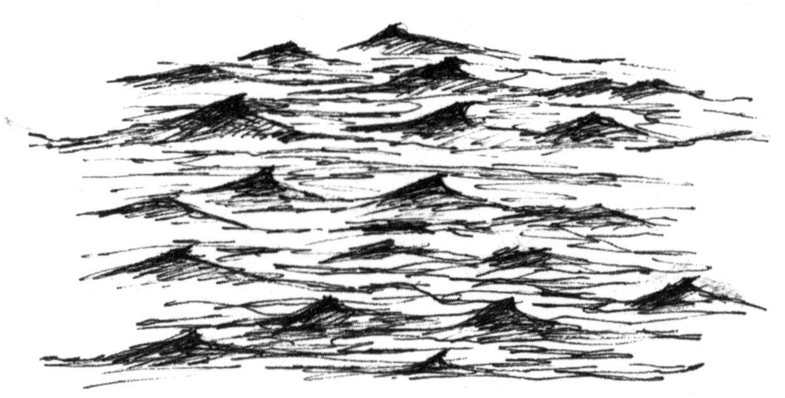

Tree bark

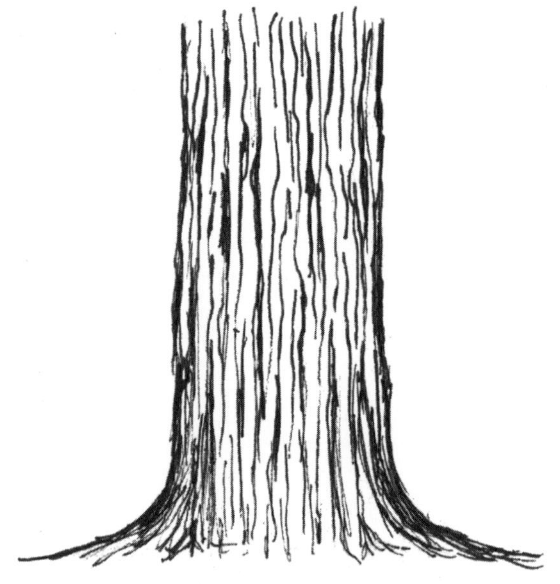

Wild grass

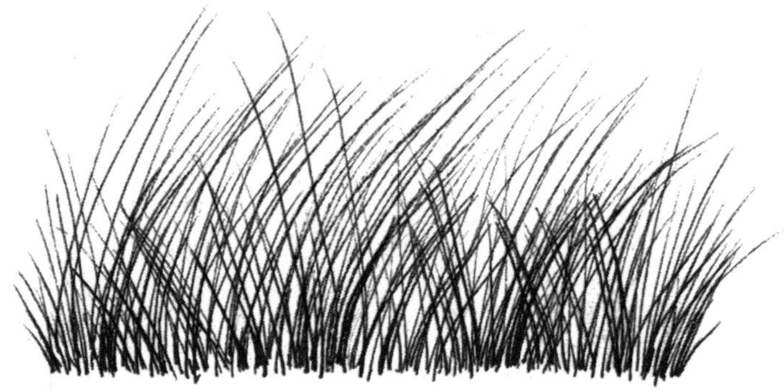

Spiky

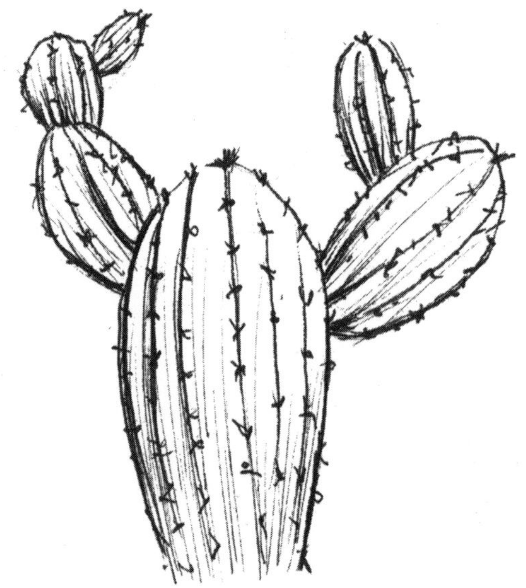

Woven fabric

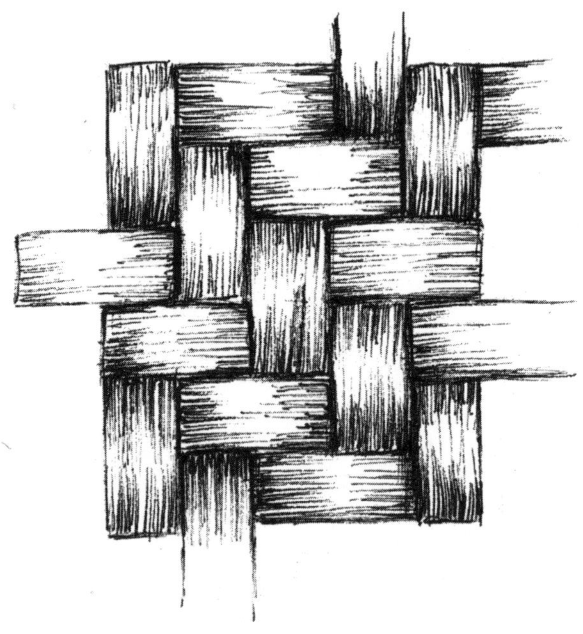

Furry

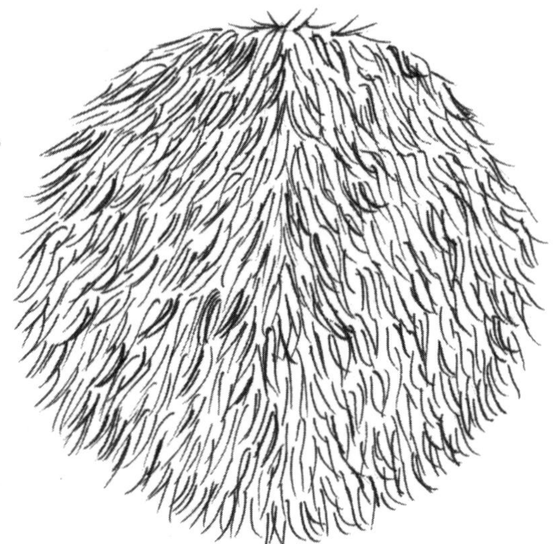

Rocky

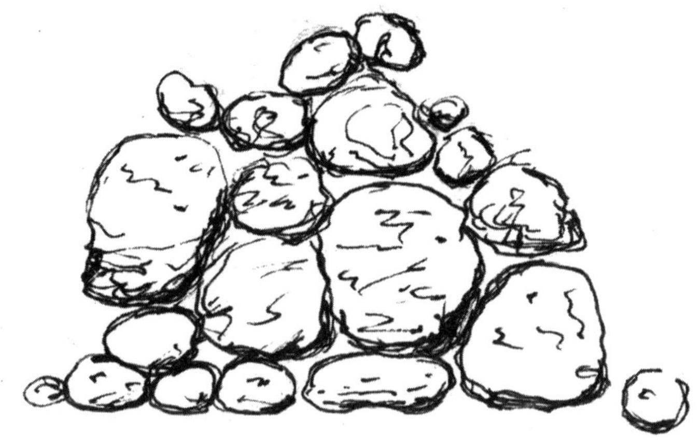

Cracked

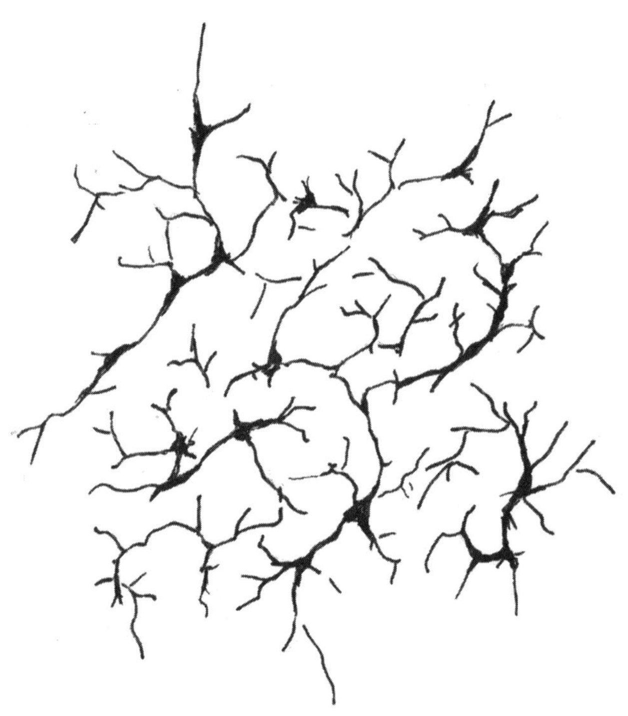

Art is not a plaything,
but a necessity . . .
a cup into which life
can be poured.

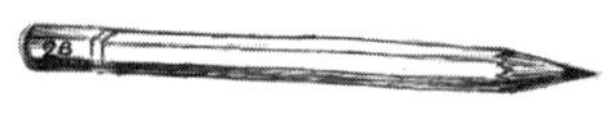

Rebecca West

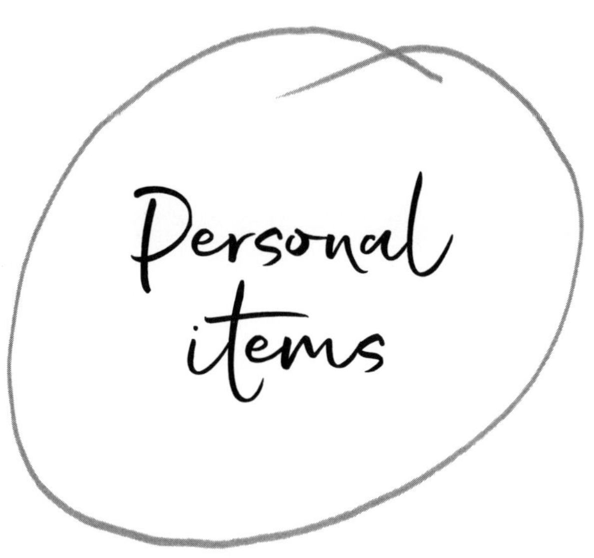
Personal items

Headphones

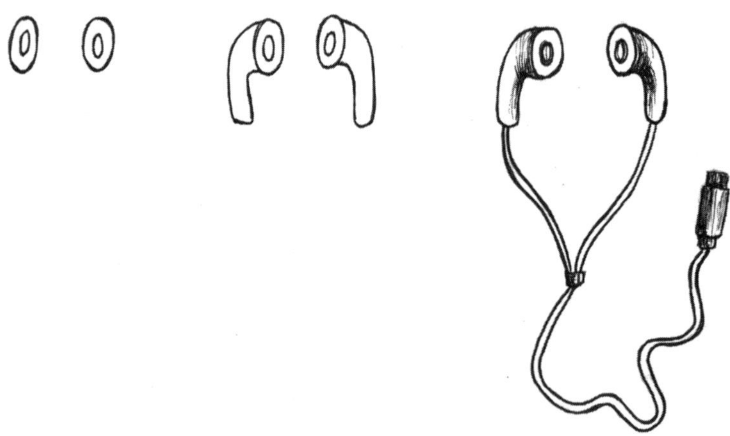

Phone

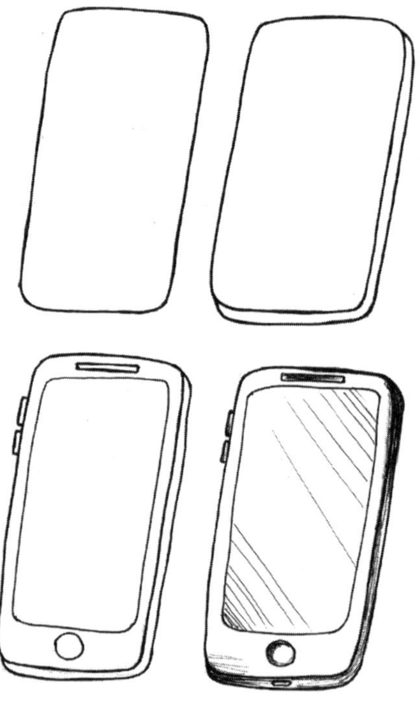

Hat

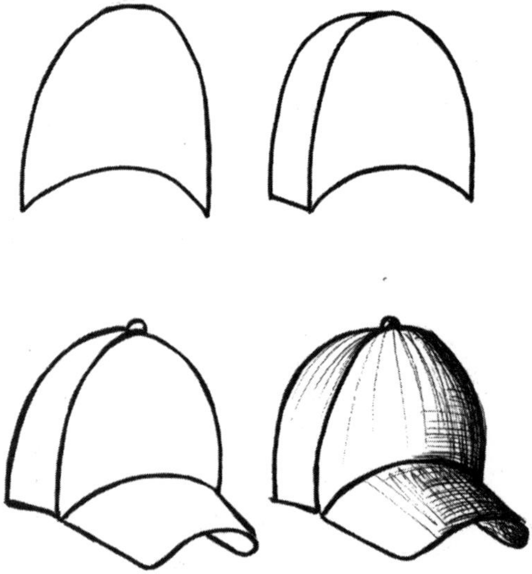

Backpack

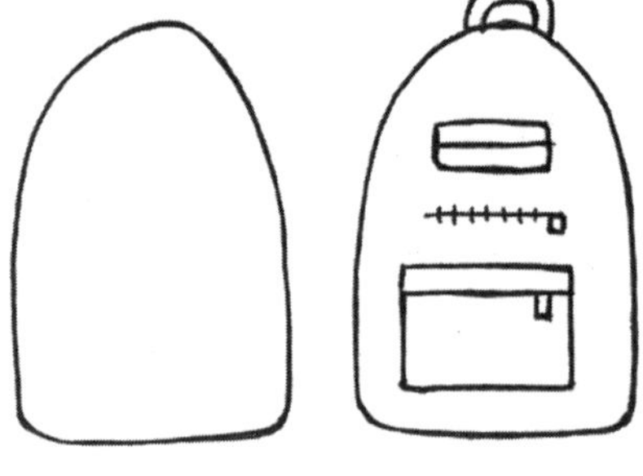

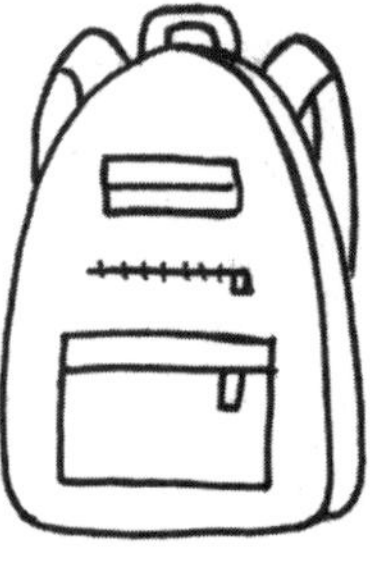

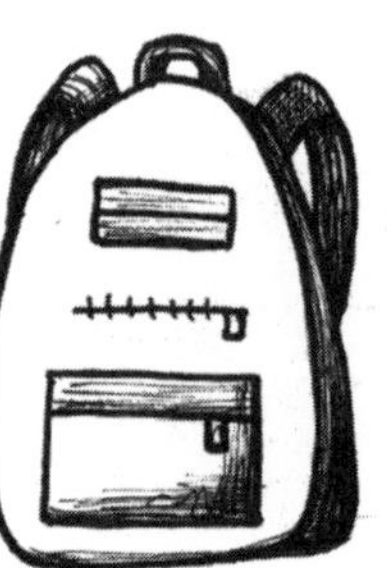

Wallet

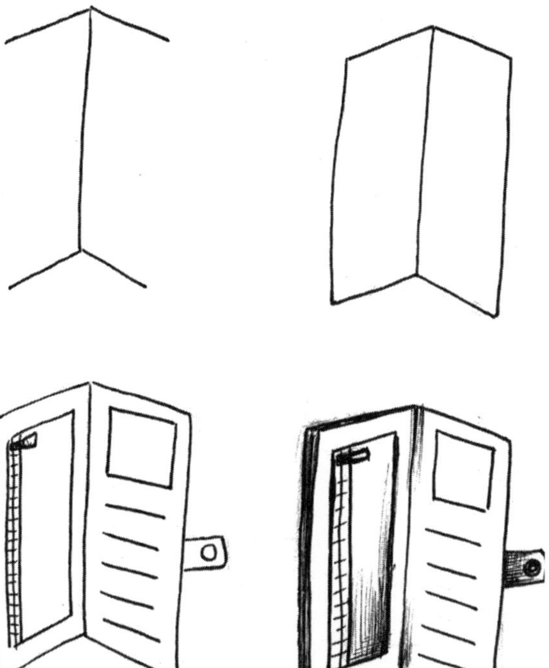

Glasses

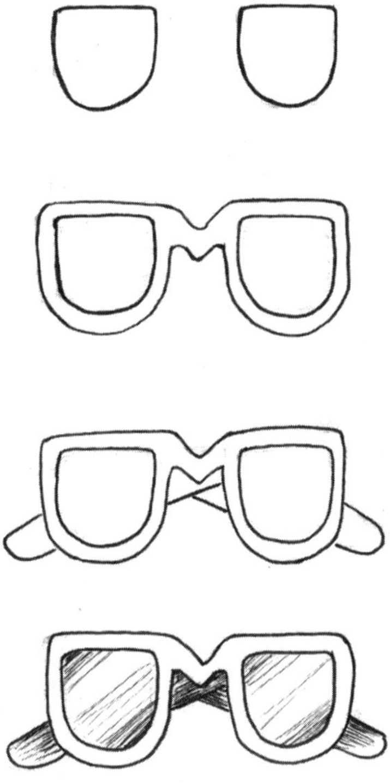

Toothbrush

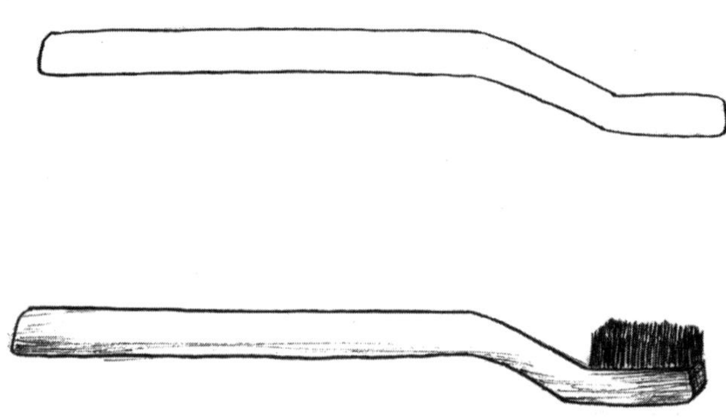

Key

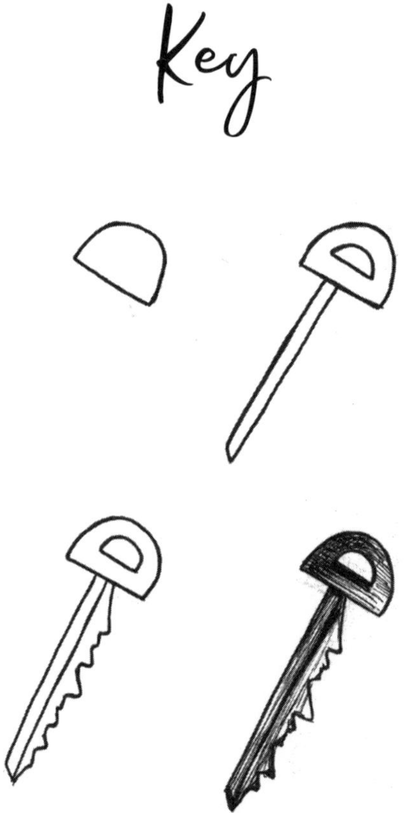

Watch

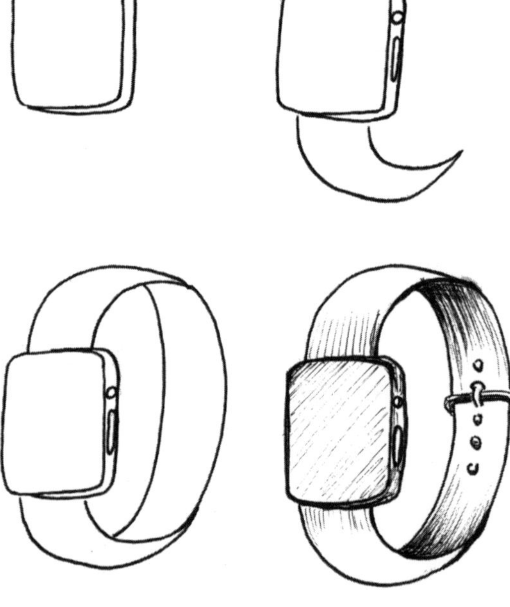

Book

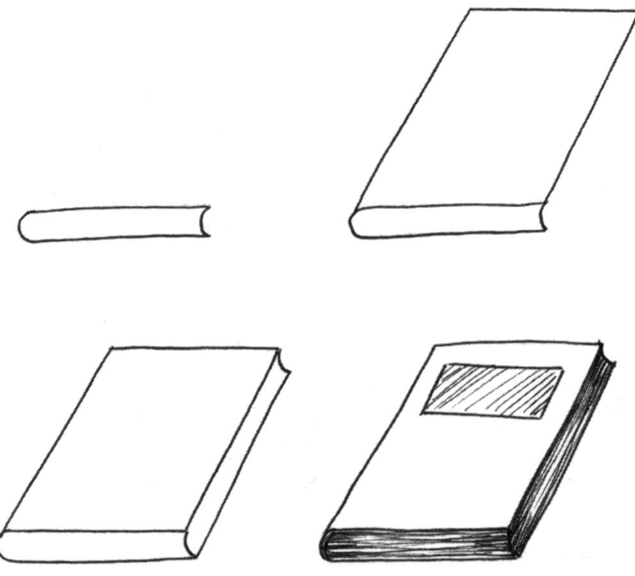

Painting is just
another way of
keeping a diary.

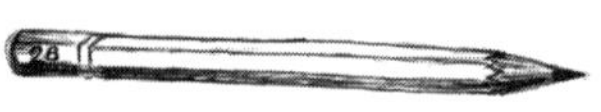

Picasso

Household items

Teapot

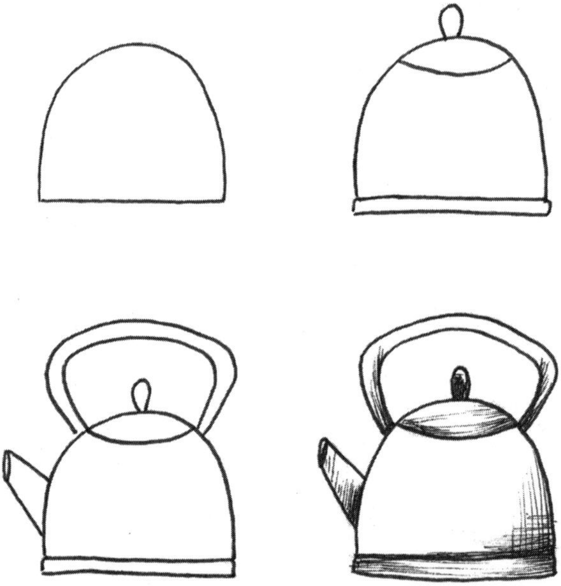

Lamp

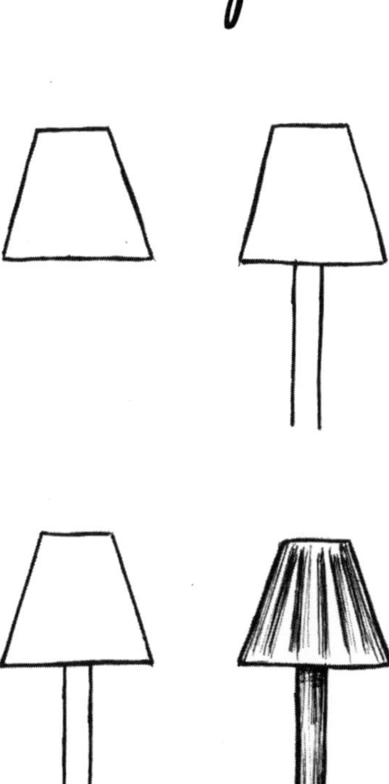

Remote control

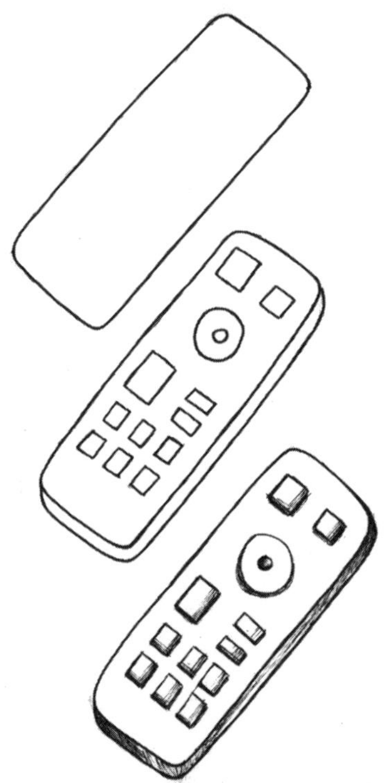

Water bottle

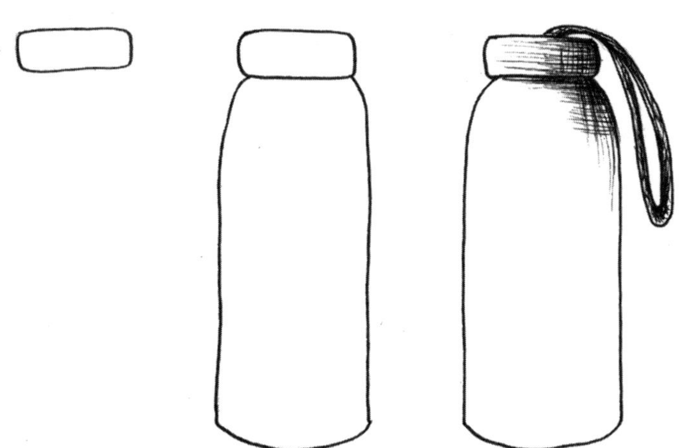

Pen

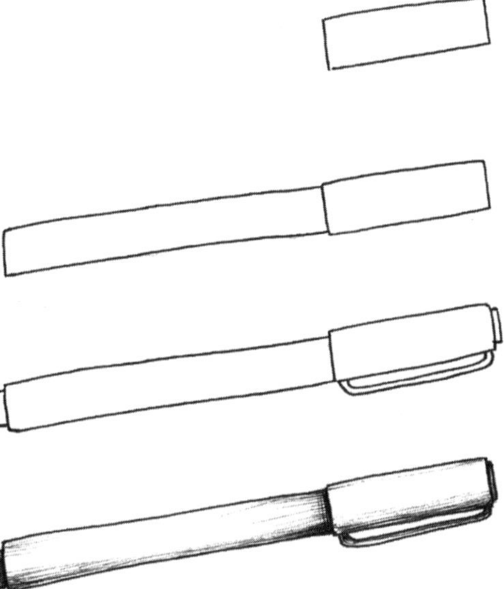

Fridge

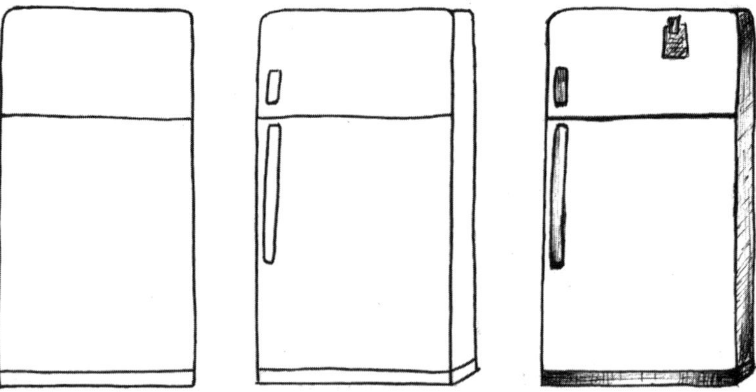

Hairbrush

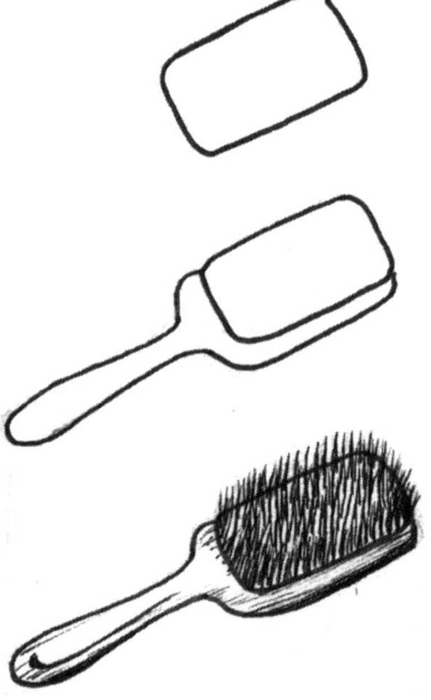

Toaster

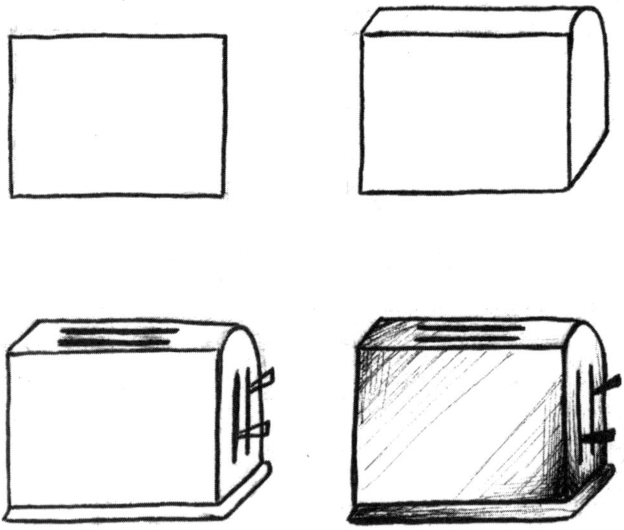

Shelf

Candle

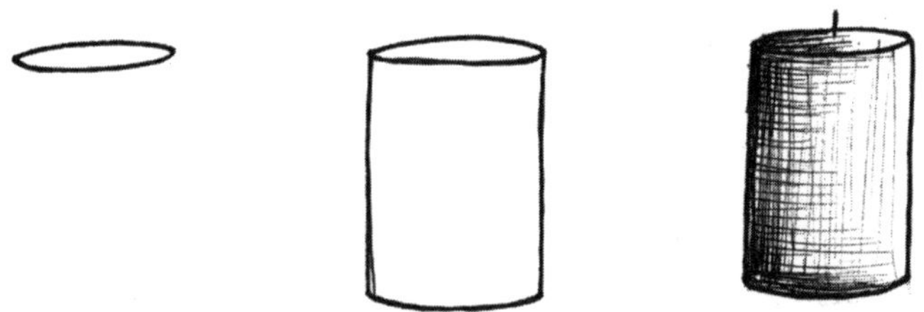

Art is expression,

not perfection.

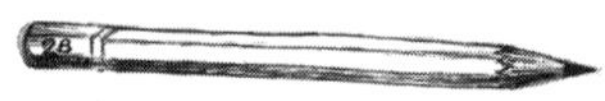

Food and drink

Bowl of cereal

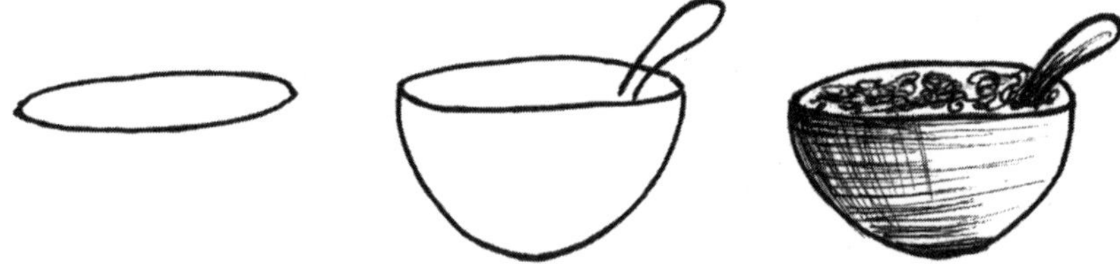

Takeaway coffee

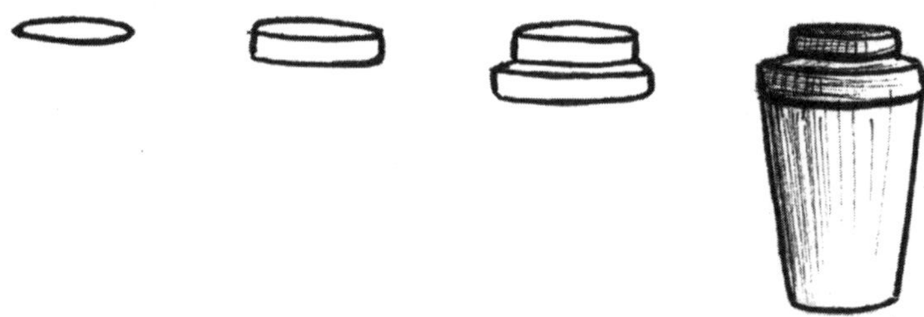

Croissant

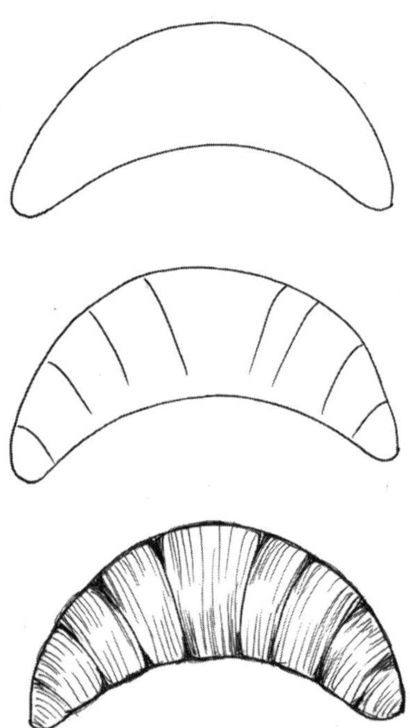

Soda

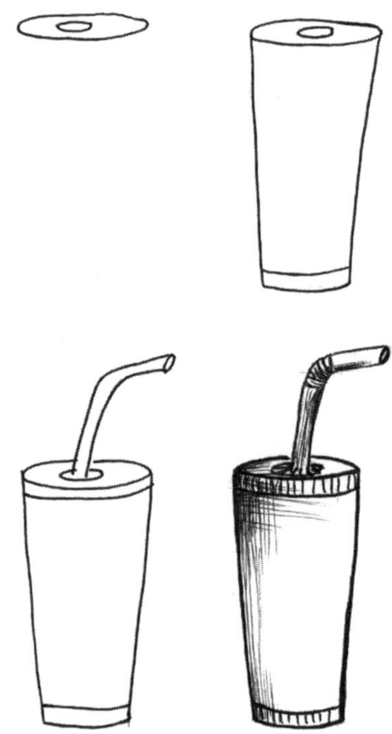

Sandwich

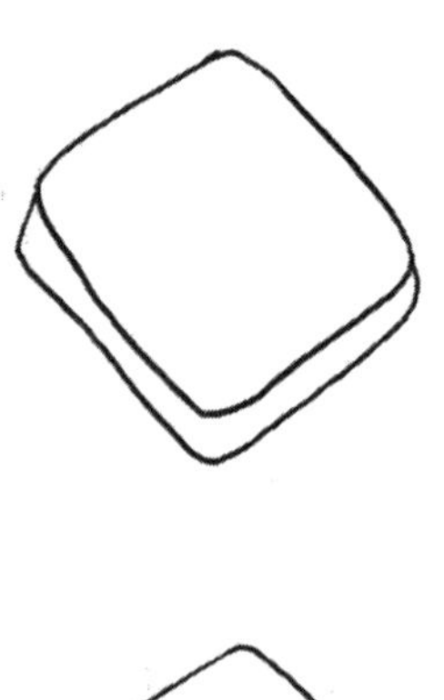 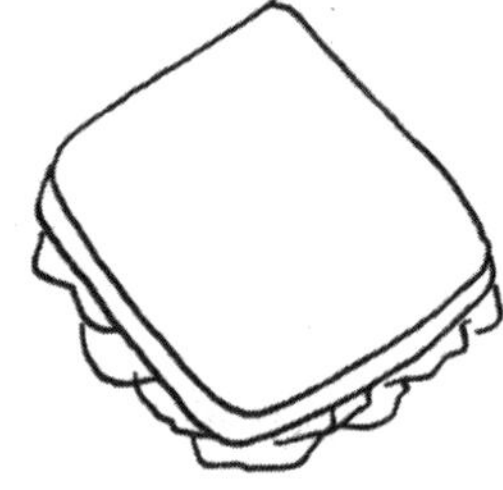

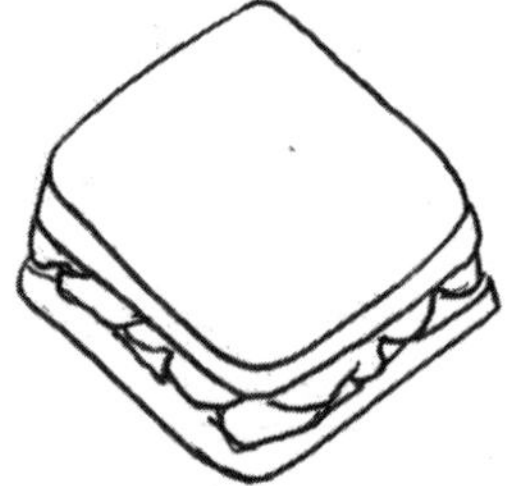 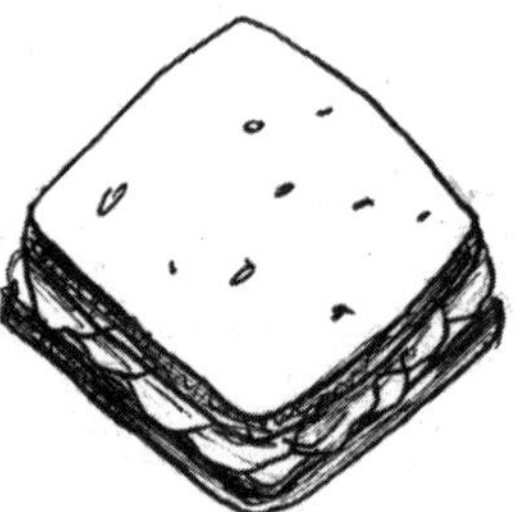

Pizza

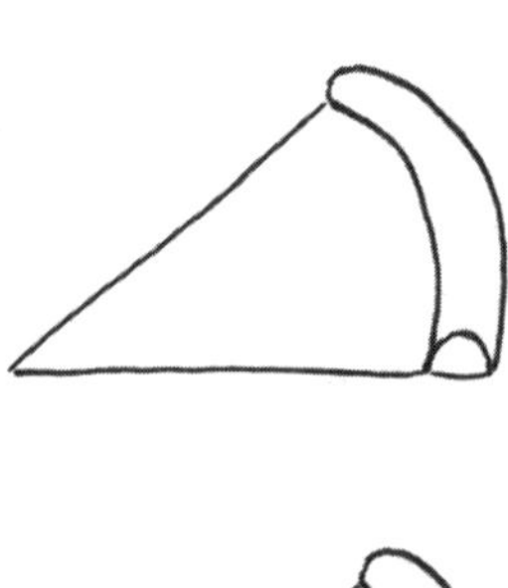

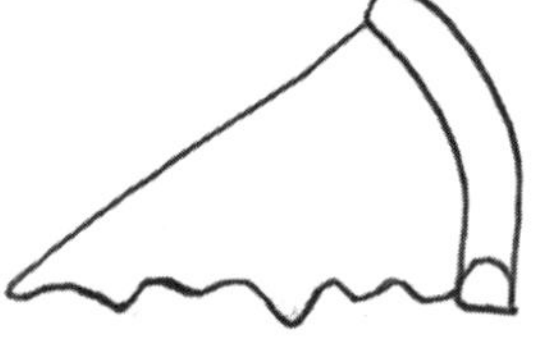

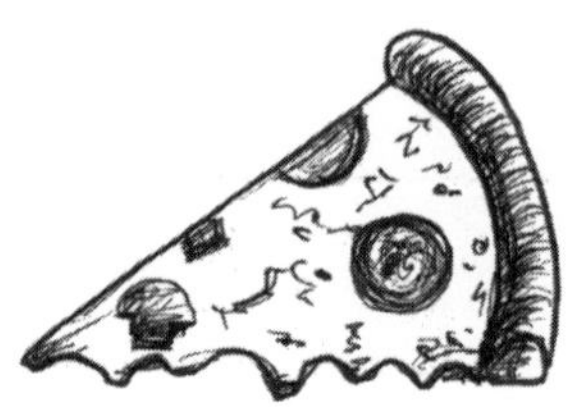

Pancakes

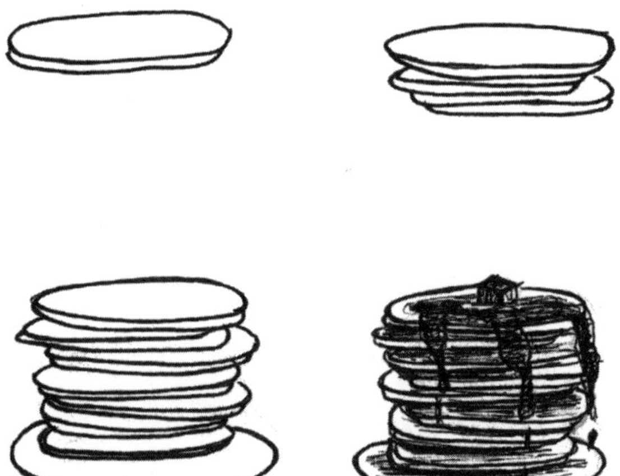

Pie

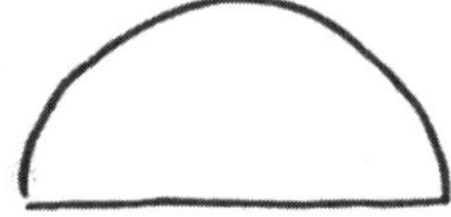

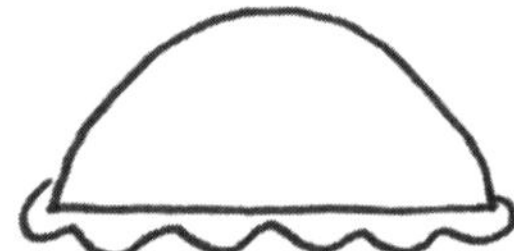

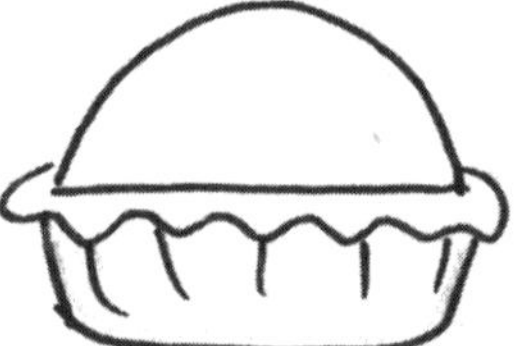

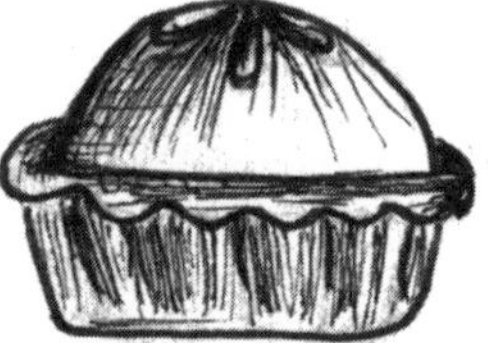

Ramen

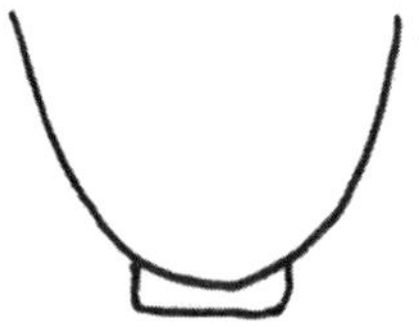 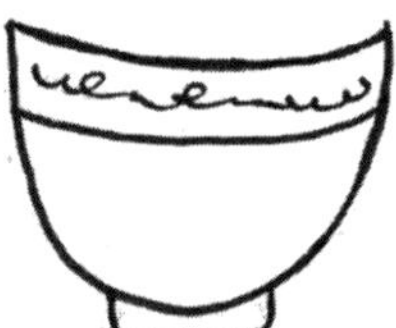

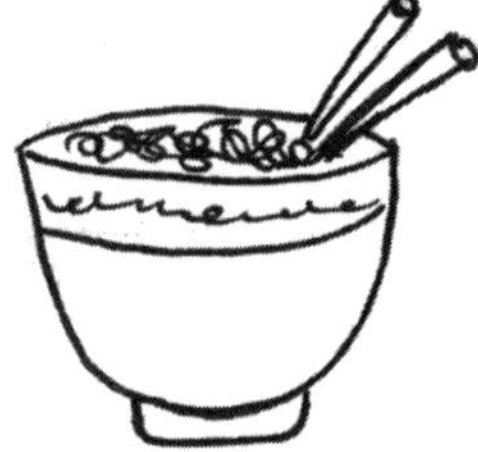 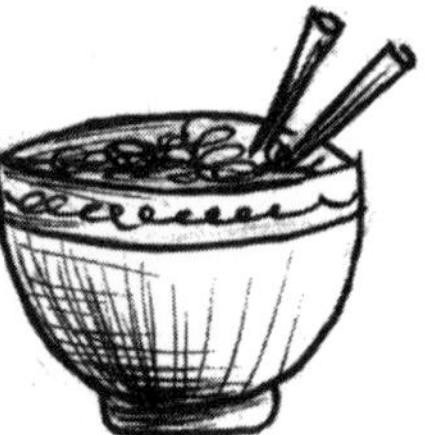

Citrus fruit

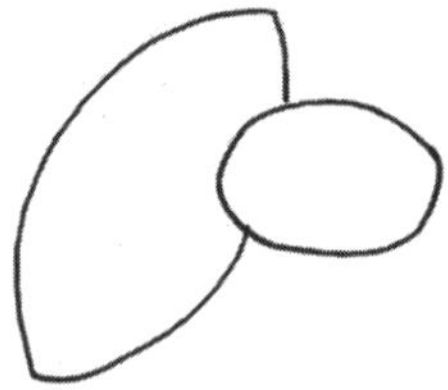

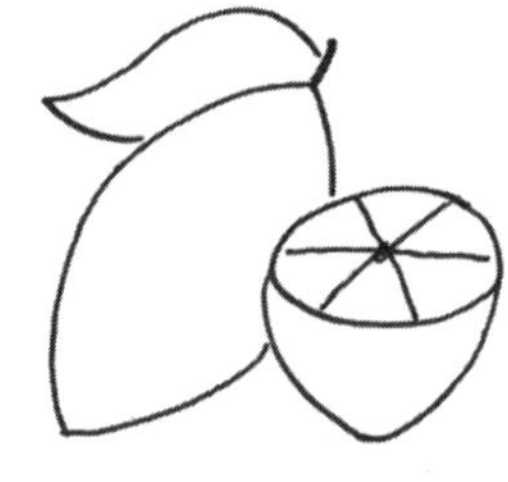

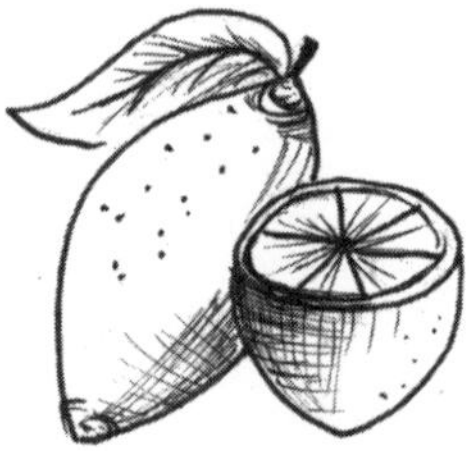

An active line
on a walk,
moving freely,
without a goal.

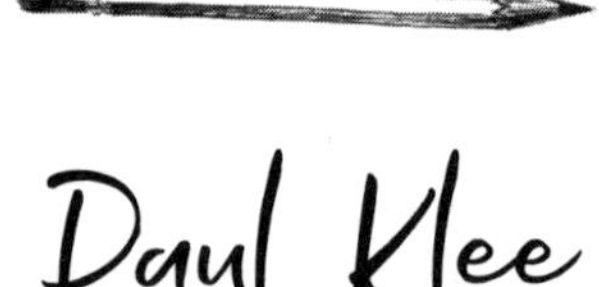

Paul Klee

Natural things

Leaves

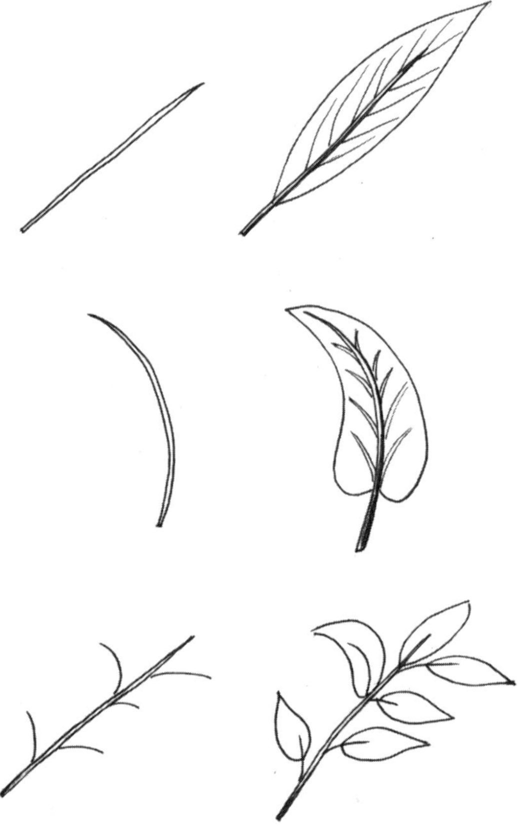

Tree

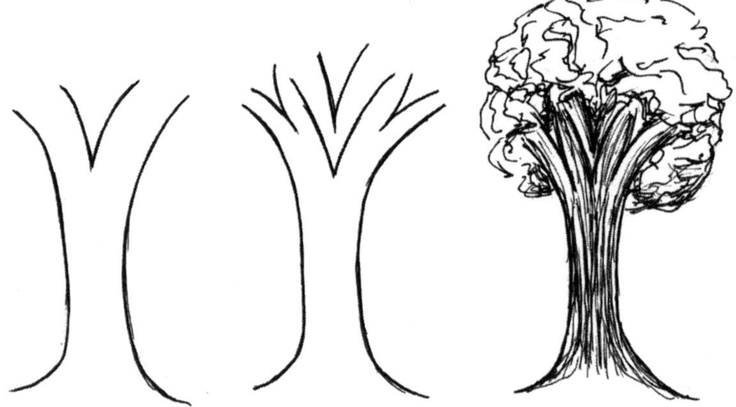

Cactus

Seashells

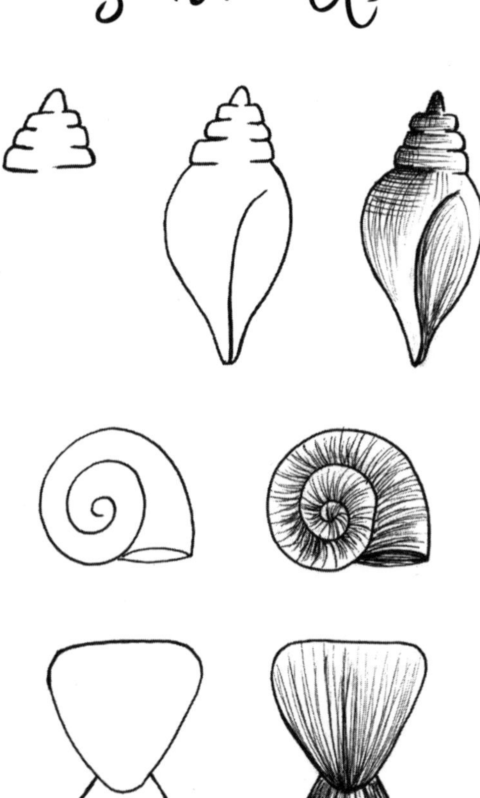

Mushrooms

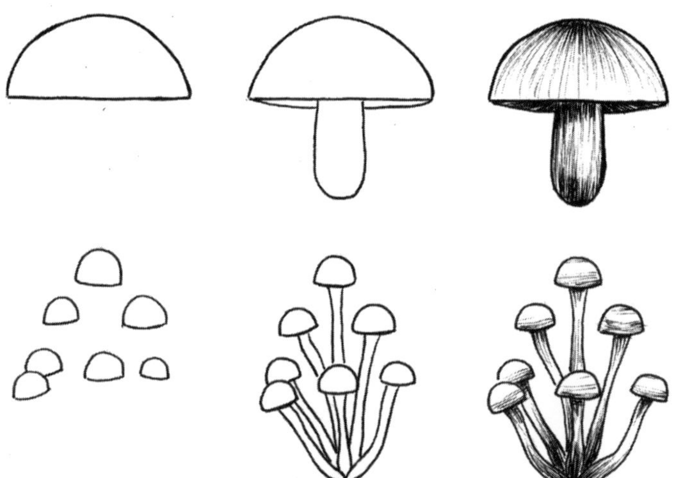

Feather

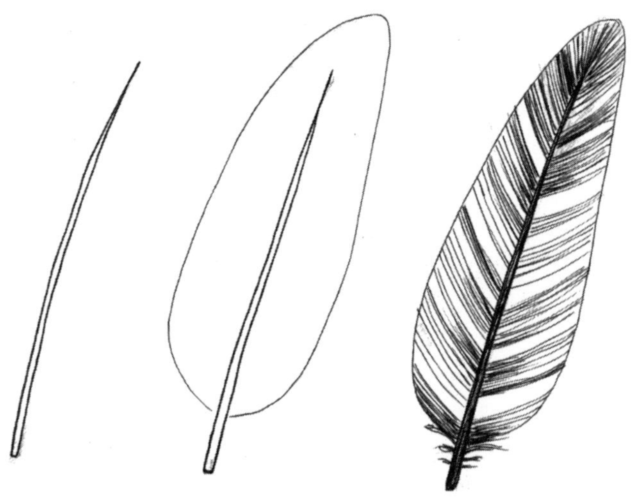

Vines on a wall

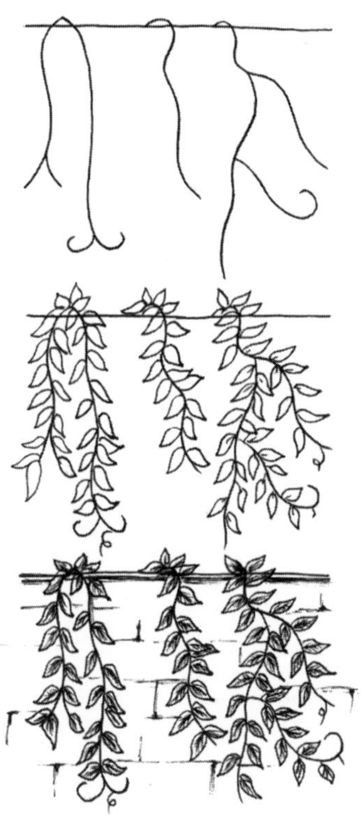

A winding river

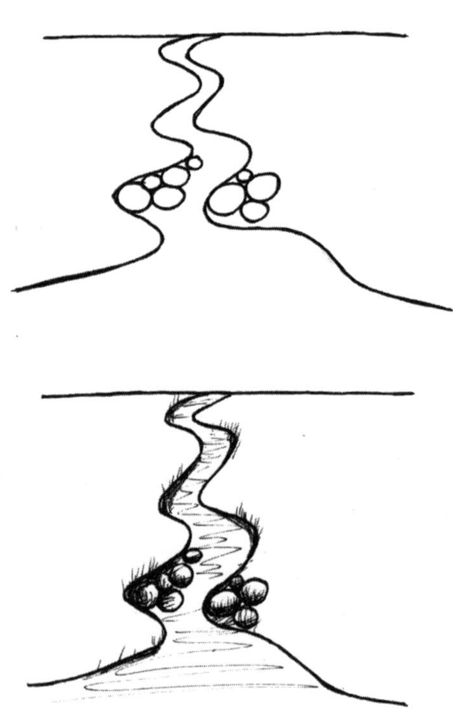

A path lined with trees

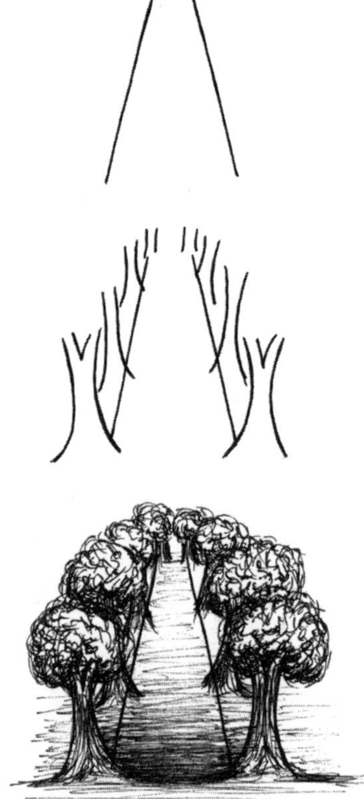

Mountain range

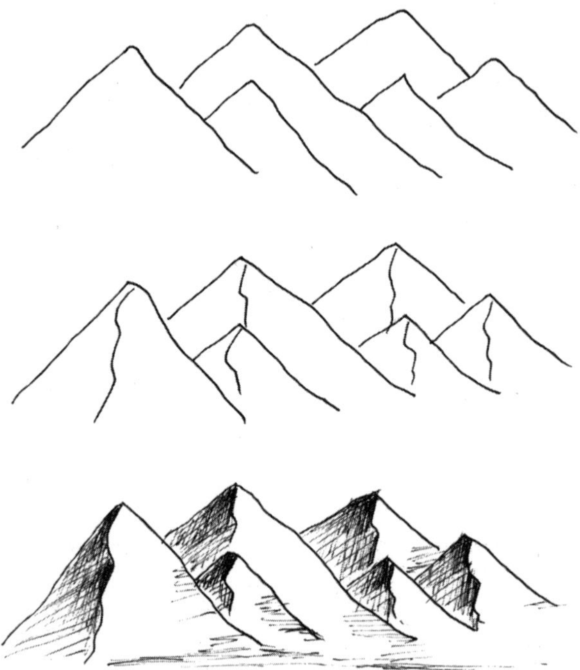

When you draw,
you let yourself
be human:
imperfect,
open and free.

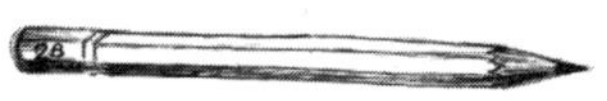

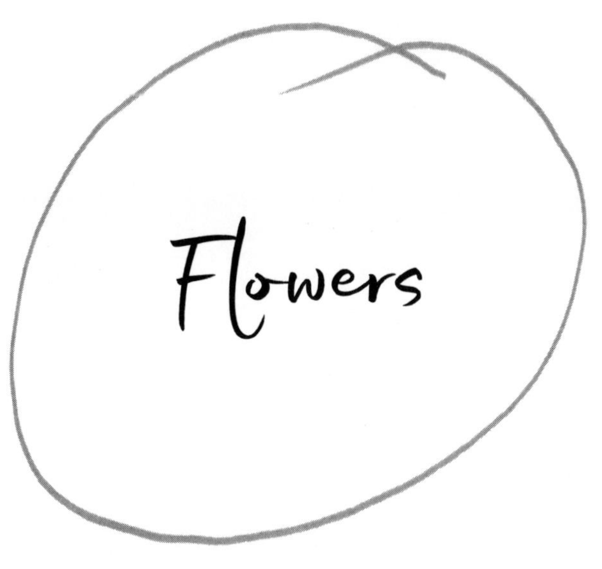

Flowers

Daisy

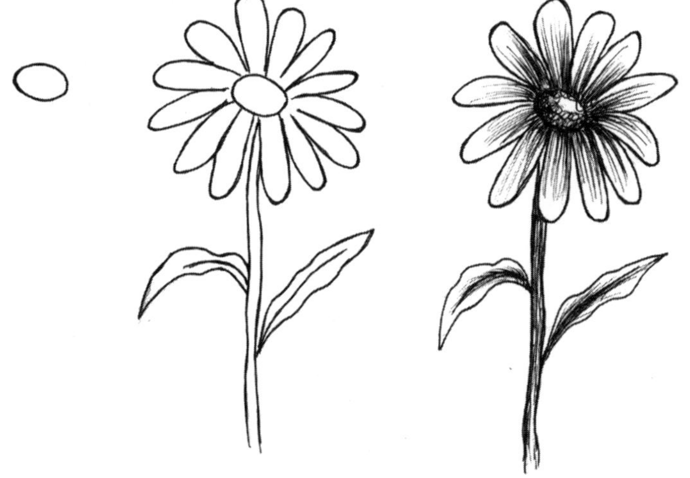

Tulip

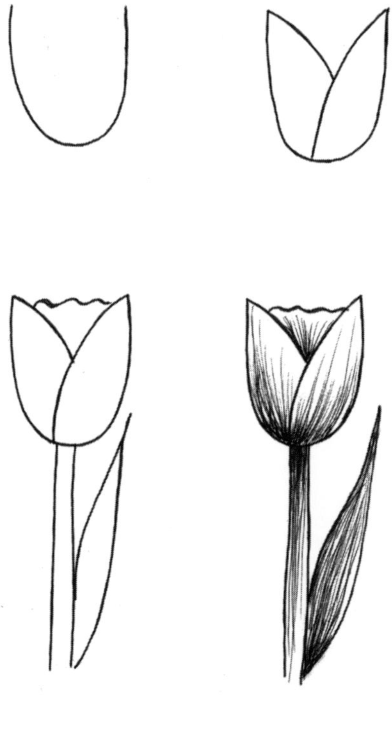

Lily

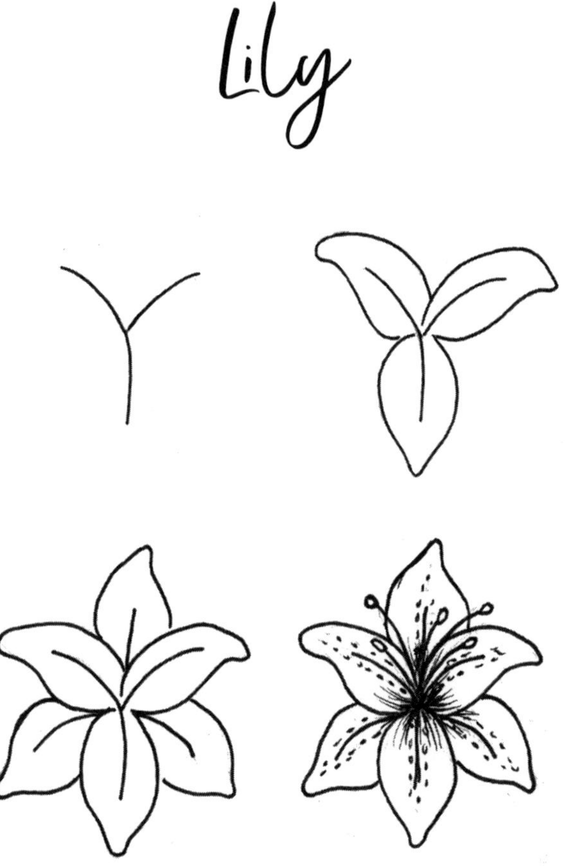

Daffodil

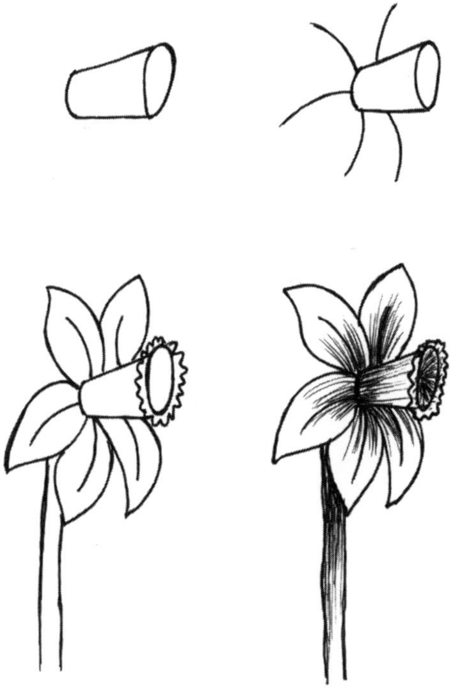

Cherry blossom

Lavender

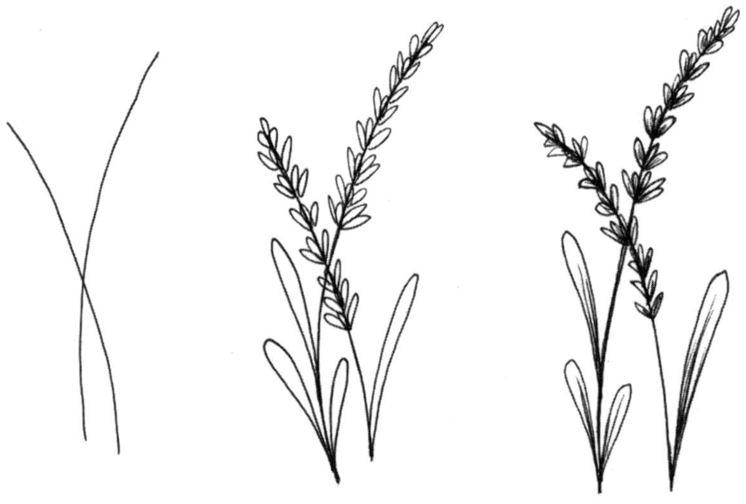

Sunflower

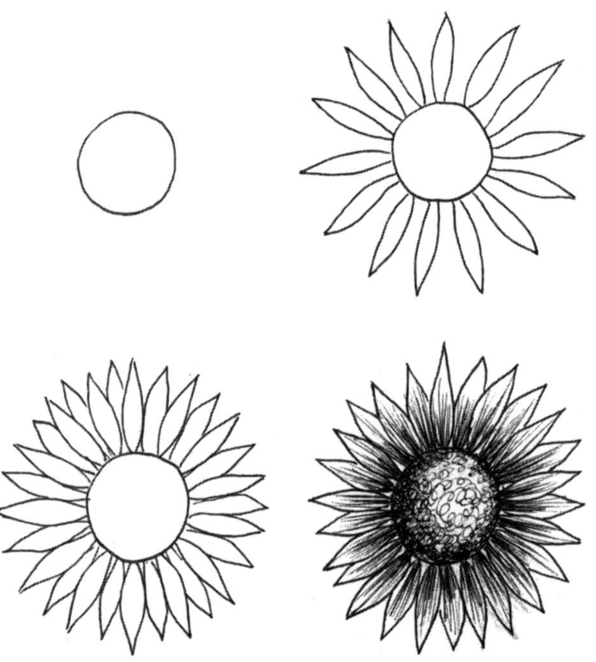

Hibiscus

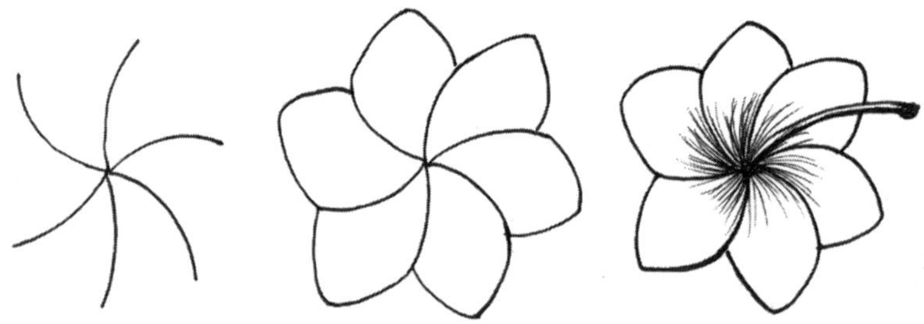

Carnation

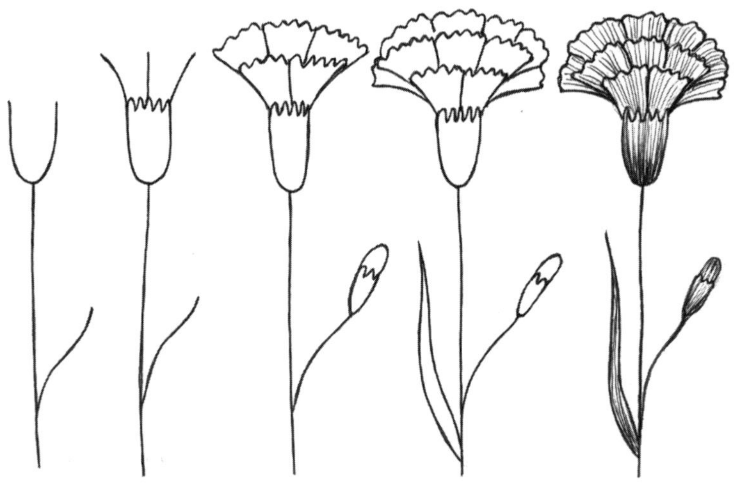

Rose

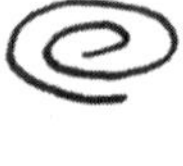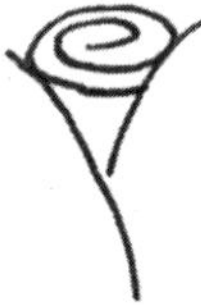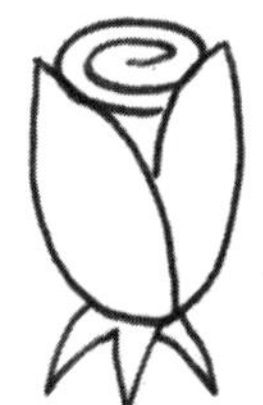

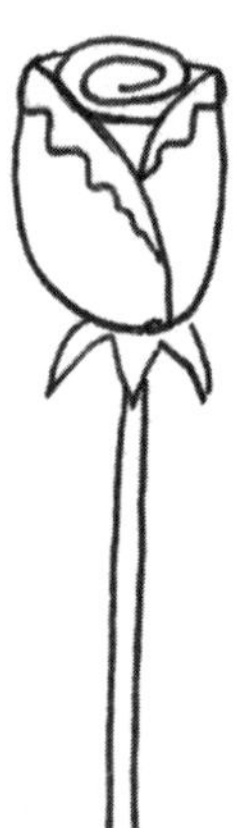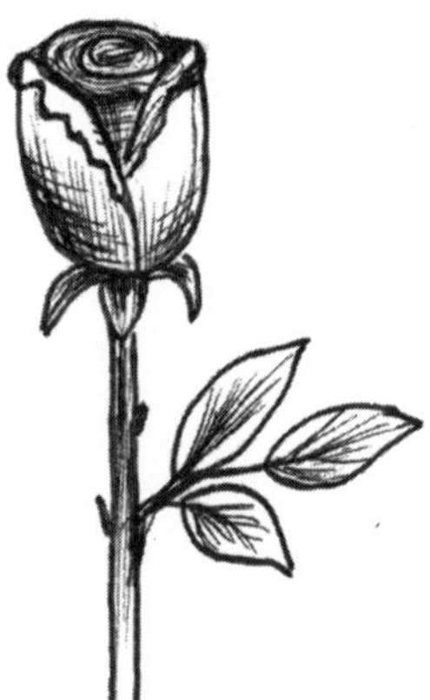

The greatest
mistake you can
make in life is to be
continually fearing
you will make one.

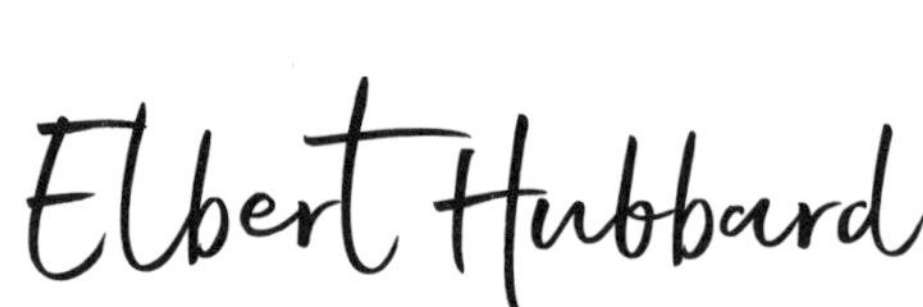

Elbert Hubbard

Urban scenes

House

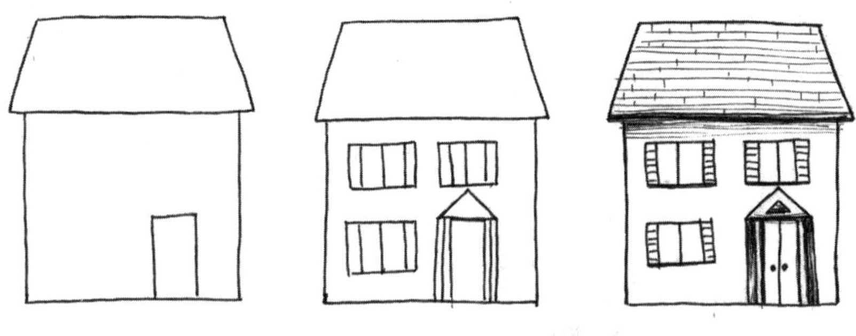

Apartment building

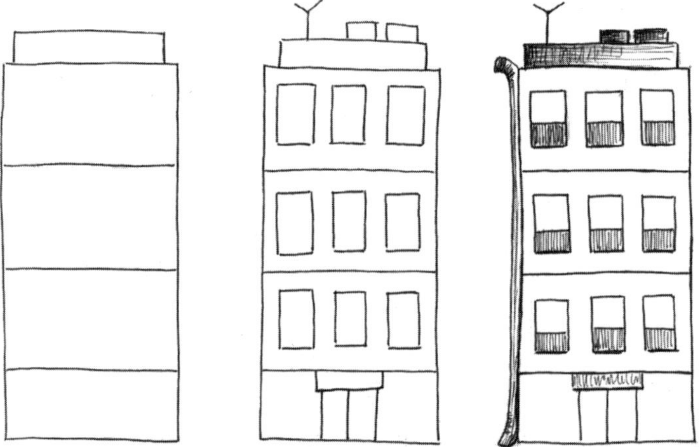

Park bench

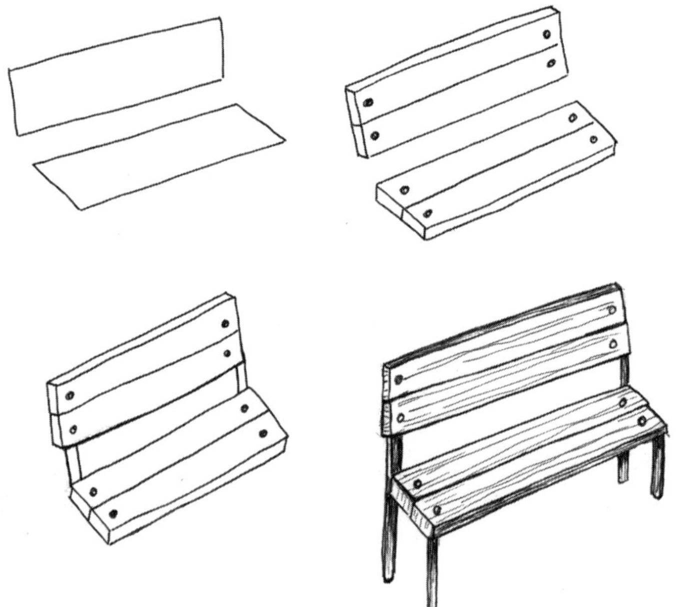

Street signs

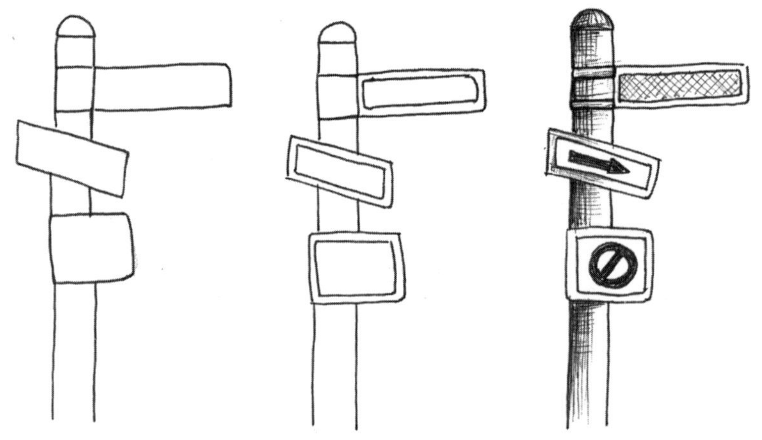

Café shop front

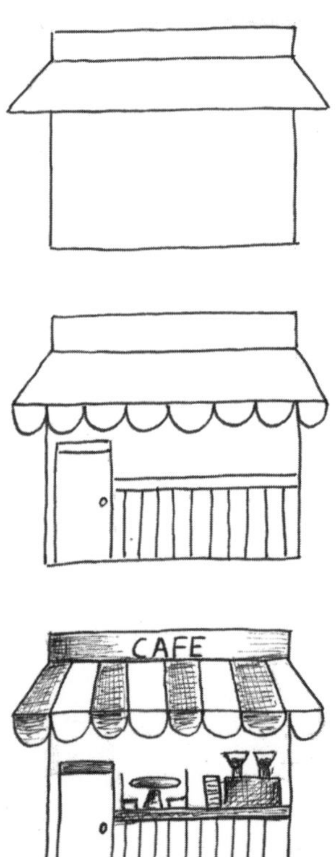

Garbage can

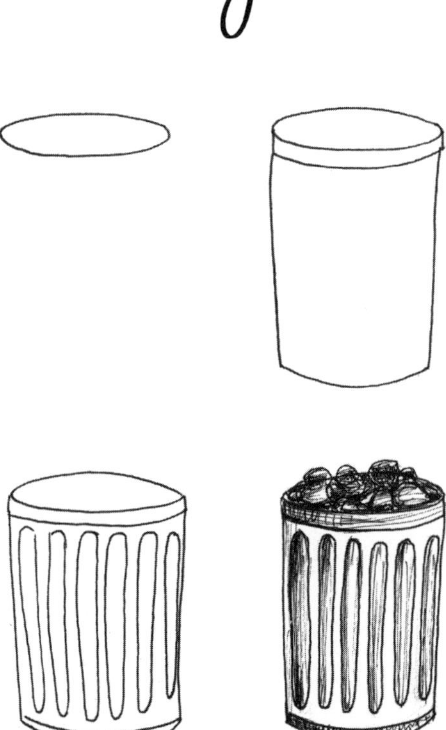

Street food truck

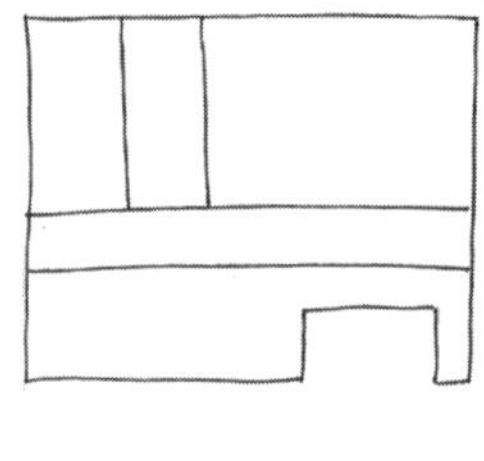

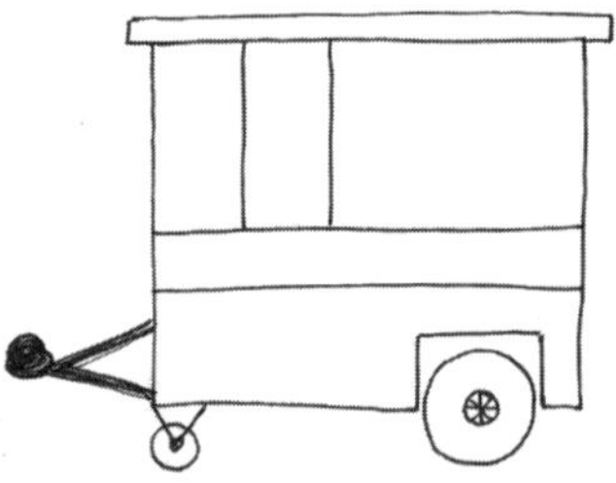

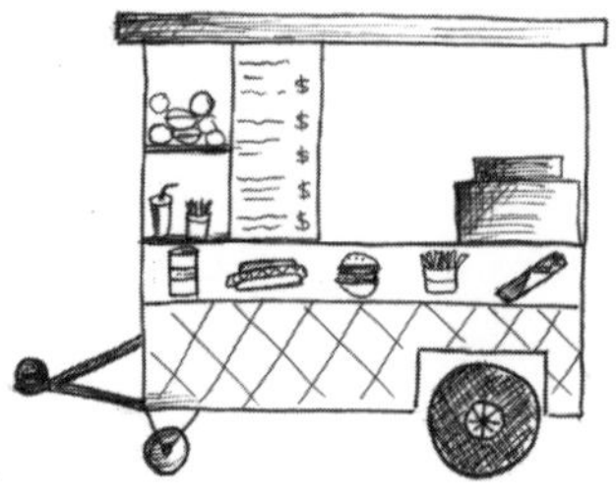

street light

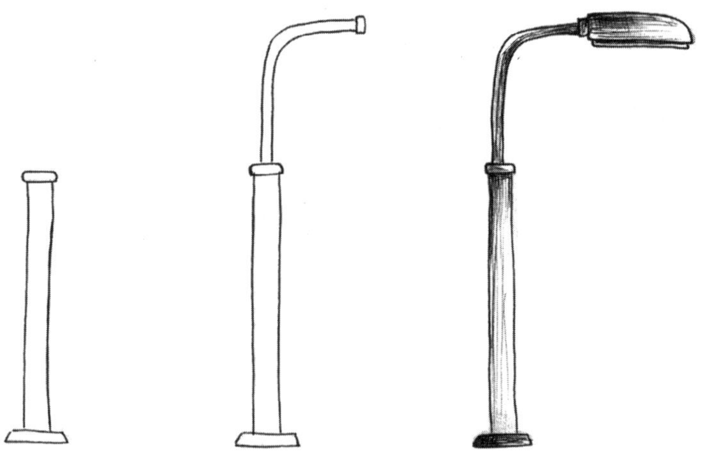

Apartment balcony

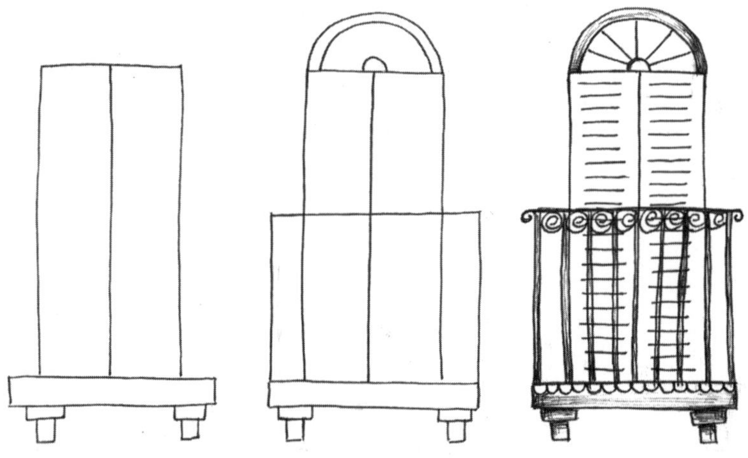

A doorway

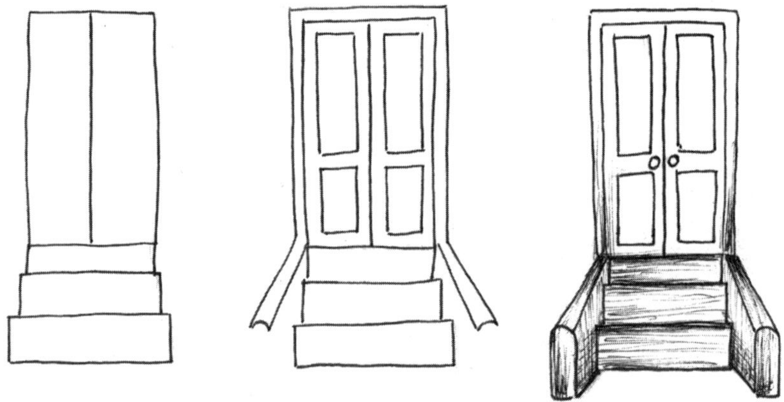

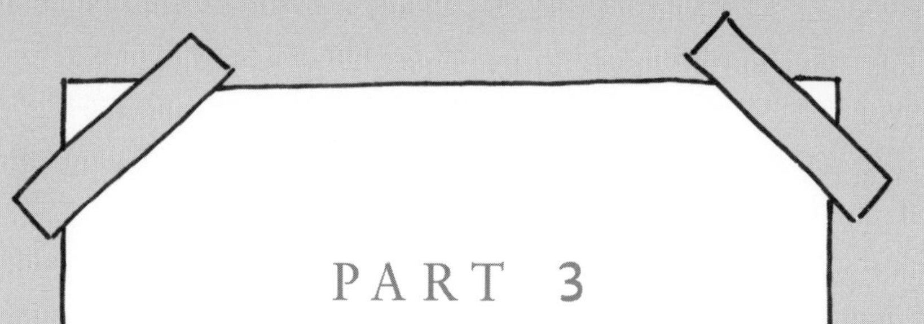

Capture *your* day

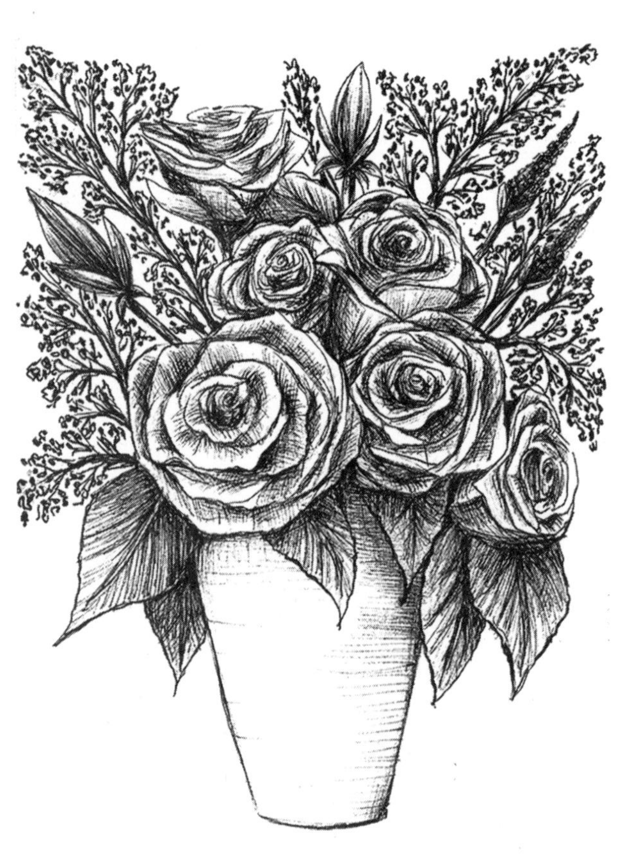

This section of the book is all about capturing moments from your day using the techniques you've learned so far. Think of it as a creative diary where you can express yourself through art.

I truly believe there is beauty in anything we observe and that anything can be used as inspiration and turned into art. There's a lot of power in tapping into your curiosity and allowing yourself the freedom to make your mark on a page. Feel free to experiment with different mediums and art styles. Use these pages to unravel your thoughts and emotions, and to explore your creative muscles.

To help you organise your ideas, it's a good approach to start your drawings in pencil and lay out the shapes and lines and then go over it with a pen or coloured markers.

Be in the moment; find beauty in the mundane.

Capture your morning

Take a moment to notice your morning surroundings and draw your observations. You could capture a physical object (such as your breakfast), the view from your window, or an activity from your morning routine.
Pick something that inspires you and start sketching.

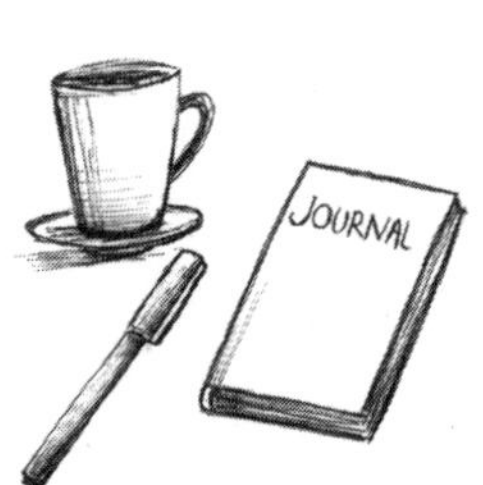

Nature *impressions*

Head outside and let nature inspire you. Gather leaves and flowers and any other textured object that catches your attention and sparks your curiosity. Sketch your collection all over this page, focusing on shapes, textures and patterns.

Texture observation

Sit in a quiet place and observe your surroundings without any distractions for a few minutes. What textures do you see that you might usually miss? Is it the woven fabric of a cushion or the grain of a wooden surface? Draw a texture that you would normally overlook or not pay attention to.

Five senses drawing

Spend a few minutes tuning into your five senses (sight, sound, touch, smell, taste) in your current environment. Create a small drawing that represents each of your sensory experiences.

Object study

Select a common object such as a cup, shoe or plant.
Observe the object closely, noting its shape, texture and details.
Create several sketches of the object from different angles.

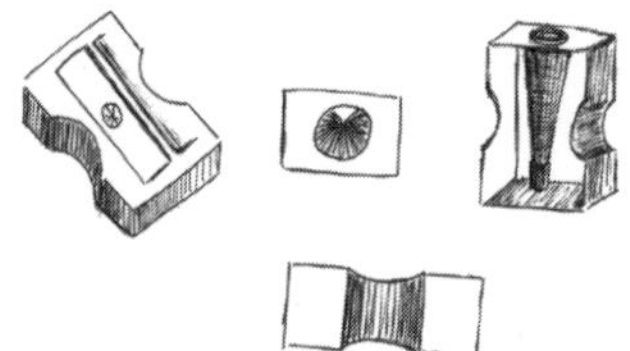

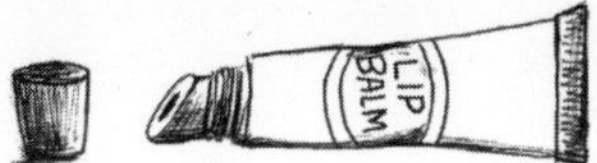

Daily *routine* object

Choose an object you use daily – a toothbrush or
a pen, for instance – and draw it in as much detail as
you can. Pay attention to its shape and texture, noting
any unusual features such as wear and tear.

A *window* view

Find a window and take in the scene outside. Draw
what you see – things like trees, buildings and the sky.
Look closely to include as much detail as possible.

Mood landscape

How are you feeling today? Imagine your mood as
a landscape – a quiet forest, a lively field or a stormy sea.
Use lines, shapes and colours to sketch what your inner
world looks like. Sketch and colour the landscape,
focusing on capturing the mood.

In-the-moment *snapshot*

Illustrate something from this present moment.
What's catching your attention right now? Maybe it's a texture,
a burst of colour or an object nearby. Whatever it is, draw
it just as it feels in this moment – a little snapshot of now.

Find your
inspiration in
the everyday.

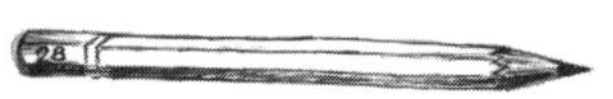

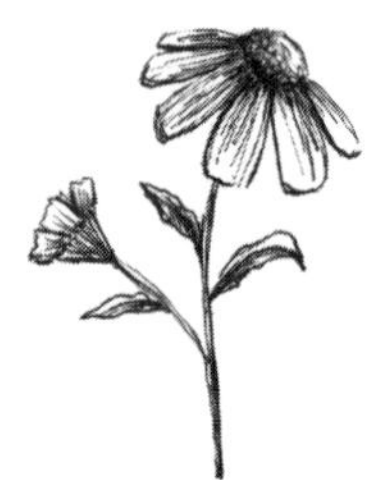

Floral *obsession*

Fill this page with florals and botanical drawings.
You can gather some flora from your garden, go for
a walk or search for some inspiration online.

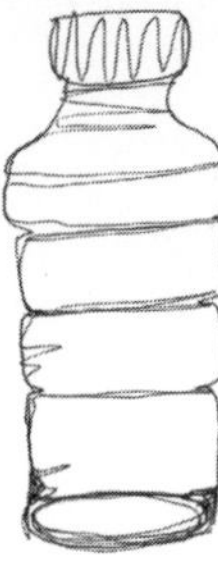

One-line drawing

Find a simple object – a leaf, a cup
or a small plant. Draw it using one
continuous line. No lifting your pen!

Take a *line* for a walk

Allow yourself a moment to be still and breathe.
Pick up a pen or pencil and let your hand create lines and
shapes, drawing freely and without thought. It's okay if
all you come up with is a squiggle on a page. Let yourself
create and draw freely without thought or judgement.
Add colour or other patterns or leave the page as it is.

Meal of the day

Think about the most memorable meal
you had today. Create an illustration of that meal,
focusing on the textures, shapes and colours.

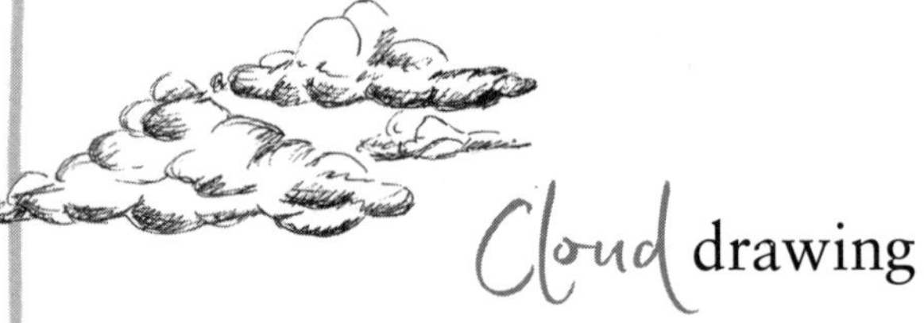

Cloud drawing

Go outside and observe some of the clouds.
What shapes do you see? Sketch their outlines and let your
imagination transform them into whatever they remind
you of – a ship, a face or just fluffy forms floating by.

Highlight of your day

Reflect on your day and identify then illustrate one
highlight. It could be as simple as your morning coffee,
or a cute dog you saw on your way to work.

I found I could say
things with color
and shapes that I
couldn't say in any
other way – things
I had no words for.

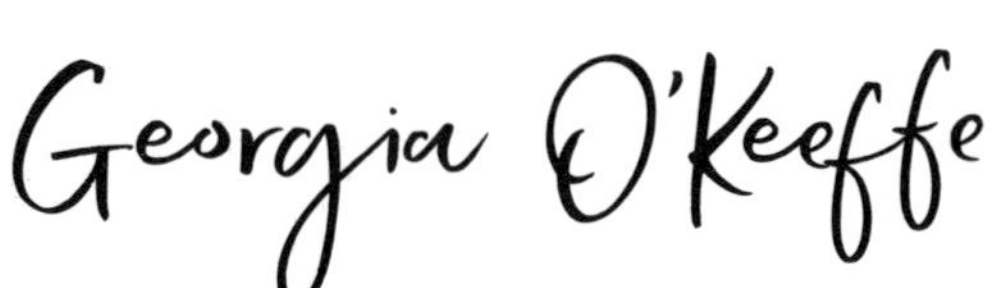

Georgia O'Keeffe

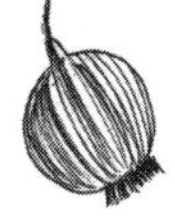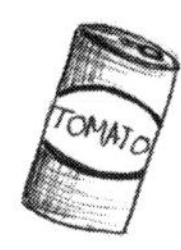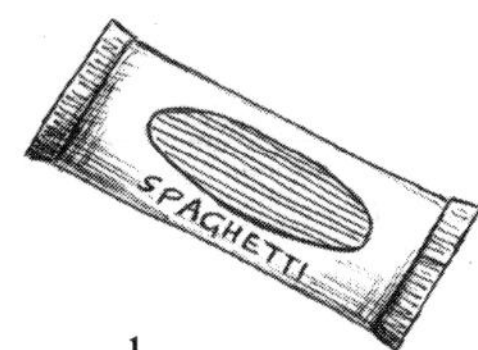

Grocery gallery

Sketch a few items from your latest grocery shop,
focusing on their shapes and details.

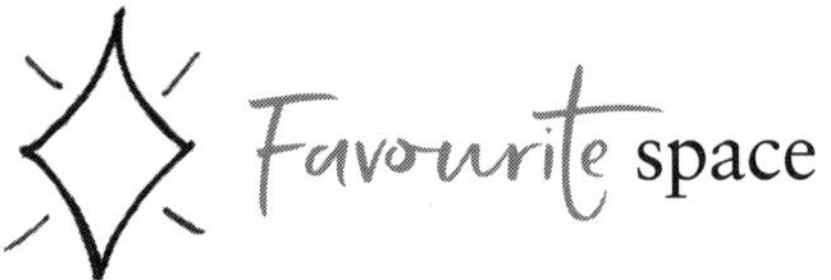

Draw a scene from your favourite space in your house, capturing the furniture, decorations and any people or pets.

Three items of *gratitude*

Identify and illustrate three things
in your day that you are grateful for.

Mindful repetition

Choose an object around you that is small enough to trace
(e.g. a key, a bottle cap or a ring) and trace its shape all over
the page. Overlap the lines and shapes and fill the page.

Celebrate the season

Design a page that captures the essence of the
current season. Include drawings of seasonal
plants, weather elements and activities.

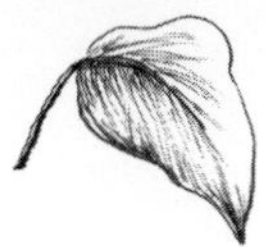

Self-care inventory

What are your favourite self-care items?
Perhaps it's your go-to mug, a face mask or
even your sketchbook. Draw one or a few,
celebrating the little things that help you recharge.

A *favourite* outfit
or accessory

Capture the details of your favourite item of
clothing or an accessory you chose for the day.

Recipe illustration

Choose a favourite recipe and illustrate
each step with drawings or diagrams. Include
ingredients, utensils and cooking techniques.

A moment of *relaxation*

What did relaxation look like for you today?
Was it a comfy chair or a moment outdoors?
Sketch the details of this moment below.

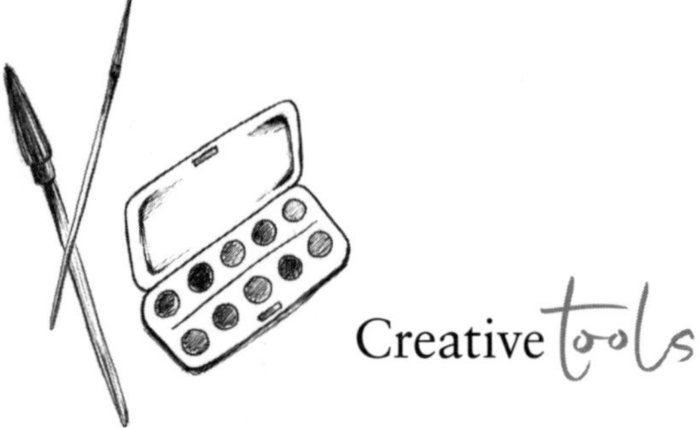

Creative tools

Draw some of the creative tools you have
been using or love to use in your art practice.

Weekly *reflection*

Use this page as your diary for the week.
Reflect on a key moment for each day
and draw one thing from that moment.

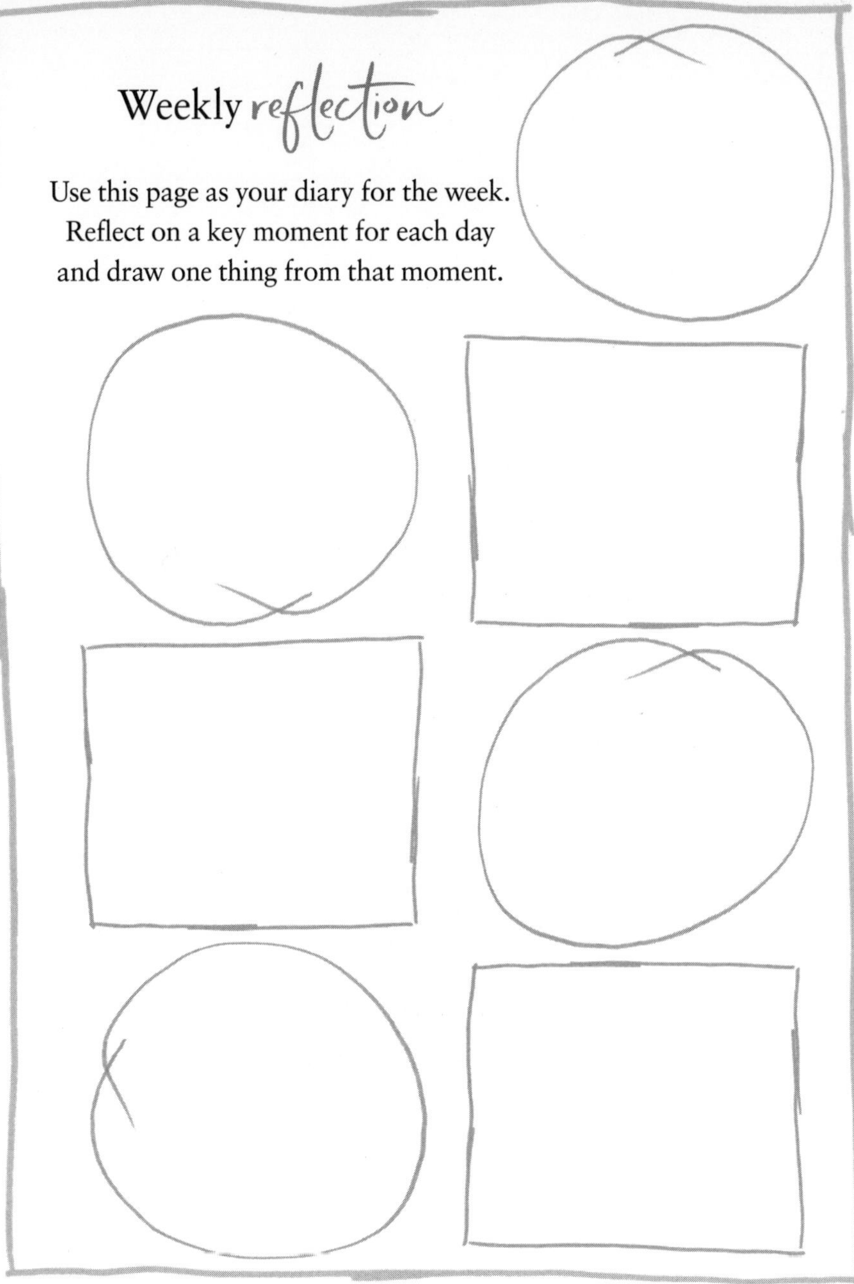

about the author

Tamara Michael is a professional artist whose work has been exhibited in numerous galleries in Australia and sold worldwide. By day she is a school teacher using doodling to bring calm to her classes after hectic lunch breaks. By night she is a TikTok star sharing her knowledge of art through accessible how-to drawing exercises, and is helping millions find calm through creativity. Tamara started her TikTok in 2020, with Instagram and YouTube following in 2021, and quickly connected with people all over the world. She is the author of *A Doodle a Day Keeps the Stress Away*.

More from Tamara Michael